Seven Card Stud
with
Seven Manangs Wild

WRITINGS ON FILIPINO AMERICAN LIVES

*Our stories unfold with
pride, joy, and love*

Evangeline Canonizado Buell

EAST BAY FILIPINO AMERICAN NATIONAL HISTORICAL SOCIETY

2002

Second Edition, October 2002
First Edition, March 2002

T'Boli Publishing and Distributor
P.O. Box 347147
San Francisco, CA 94134
e-mail: tiboli@mindspring.com

Cover Art: Lewis Suzuki
Cover and Text Design and illustrations: Carl Angel

Senior Editor: Helen C. Toribio
Managing Editors: Teresita Cataag Bautista, Evangeline Canonizado Buell,
              Elizabeth Marie Mendoza Megino
Production: Eduardo Datangel

This book was made possible by grants from the City of Berkeley Arts Commission.

ISBN 1-887764 -55-0

Library of Congress Cataloging-in-Publication Data

Seven Card Stud with Seven Manangs Wild: an anthology of Filipino-American
writing / edited by Helen C. Toribio – ed.
p.cm.

ISBN 1-887764 -55-0
1. Filipino American literary collections. 2. Art – Suzuki, Lewis
3. Illustrations – Angel, Carl 4. Title

*Lewis Suzuki's painting on the back and front cover symbolizes our immigrant parents
departure from the Philippines and arrival at the San Francisco Presidio in the early
1900's.*

Printed in Korea

ALAY
Sa aming mga magulang,
mga kabiyak ng puso at mga anak,
mga manang at manong,
at sa lahat ng aming mga kapatid.

DEDICATION
To our parents,
our spouses – the other half of our hearts,
and our children,
our elders,
and all our relations.

KABABAIHAN

WOMEN

It's been said that if you want to get the work done, get the women to do it. This book is proof. Vangie Buell, our chapter president, made sure all the stories were in. Liz Megino, who videotaped every work session, made sure each story was typed onto floppy disks along with the biographies and glossary. And Terry Bautista, our vice-president, made sure the project moved along. All three women made sure this book was funded. All four of us read each story over and over. Together we edited each piece. Our women's collective, our kababaihan, followed a long-standing tradition among Filipino American women: gathering around the table to eat, drink, gossip, work, support each other, and have fun. This scene is played out over and over, in different ways, by different families, in the stories that you'll read in this book. We hope that you'll enjoy them as much as we did.

Co-editors
Evangeline Canonizado Buell
Elizabeth Megino
Terry Bautista
Helen C. Toribio

Maraming Salamat

Many thanks to the family, the clan and the village for their support: Bill Buell, Honofre (Frank) Megino, Mel and Belle Orpilla, the San Francisco Bay Area FANHS Consortium, Beyond Lumpia & That Bamboo Dance, the Central Valley FANHS, National FANHS, Berkeley Mayor Shirley Dean, Mary Suzuki, our kapatid at Pusod, and Filipinos for Affirmative Action, the University of San Francisco Masters in Writing Program.

Our special thanks to the City of Berkeley Arts Commission. Their two-year support of this project made possible the completion of this book.

The editors gratefully acknowledge *Filipinas Magazine* for pioneering the publication of two of our stories *Seven Card Stud with Seven Manangs Wild* and *A Pickle for the Sun,* and *Writing for Our Lives* which published *New Country.*

CONTENTS

WHAT ARE YOU

CONTENTS

URBAN PINOY

On Language and the Filipino American
BROKEN ENGLISH, BROKEN PILIPINO

Helen C. Toribio

Like many children of immigrant parents, Filipino Americans raised in the United States grew up with multiple languages: the native languages of their parents and elders, the standard English spoken in schools, the street language of youth, and the dialects of imperfections born out of the inevitable mixtures of different tongues. For some of us, our first spoken words were Filipino. Others grew up speaking English sprinkled with the Americanized intonations of Filipino words. And for many, our lessons in the Filipino languages came in the form of disciplinary actions accompanied by angry words that spilled out of our parents' mouths.

We have mined our memories to illustrate in words our life journeys as Filipino Americans. These journeys span seventy years. We wrote these stories in the language that now comes naturally to us. However, to rely entirely on English would be denying an integral aspect of the American sub-culture where we were raised. We thus integrated those words we heard or overheard during adult happy hours or when our butts were stung and our arms pinched by parental sanctions.

But if childhood memories are more sentiments than replicas of past events, then defectiveness is natural. The Tagalog, Cebuano, and Ilokano words that you will find in the following pages may not be grammatically correct in the present standards of the Filipino languages. We, therefore, beg the indulgence and forgiveness of our immigrant brothers and sisters, and all relations in our ancestral homeland who have sustained the languages of our roots.

Note: 'Filipino' and 'Pilipino' are used here interchangeably.

Introduction
FILIPINO AMERICAN LIVES:
A MULTICOLORED FABRIC

=========== *James Sobredo* ===========

When I arrived in the San Francisco Bay Area eleven years ago, Filipinos in the East Bay welcomed me with open arms. They were filled with excitement from attending the 1990 Filipino American National Historical Society (FANHS) conference in Sacramento and had wanted to form an East Bay chapter of FANHS. Evangeline (Vangie) Canonizado Buell and her husband Bill welcomed us to their lovely home in the Berkeley hills. Among the people gathered at the meeting were Helen Caubalejo Toribio and Abraham (Abe) F. Ignacio, Jr., Elizabeth (Liz) Mendoza and Honofre (Frank) Salvador Megino, Anita Escandor and Ben Nobida, and Teresita (Terry) Cataag Bautista. In a few months, the East Bay group would be a chartered branch member of FANHS.

Over the years I developed a cherished friendship with many of the East Bay FANHS members. As a colleague in the Ethnic Studies Department at UC Berkeley where she worked as an undergraduate advisor, Liz Megino became my close friend and source of much needed encouragement. Vangie Buell formed the other half of my UC Berkeley support system. As Events Coordinator for the International House, Vangie provided the most diverse international events that my wife Lou and I have ever attended. Throughout all these years, Vangie, who also serves as our East Bay FANHS President, has graciously continued to open her home to us for our regular historical society meetings.

Terry Bautista has changed my intellectual perspective on Filipino American history by poignantly reminding me that, contrary to what some scholars argue, the Asian American movement and social protests were not all centered in the great metropolis of San Francisco. This theme played itself out in a strange twist several years later when Helen Toribio and I were comrades during a Filipino American protest of a 1998 book award given by the Association for Asian American Studies at their annual conference in Hawaii. Filipino Americans felt the book reinforced racist stereotypes of Filipinos in Hawaii. Helen, my wife Lou and I were in Honolulu as East Bay FANHS members who protested against the book award.

Writing this "Introduction" reminds me of NVM Gonzalez, a dear friend and intellectual inspiration. NVM also spent the majority of his time in America living in the East Bay community of Hayward where he taught literature at California State University. NVM rejected the view that Filipinos must choose between the Philippines and America—he lived and traveled comfortably in both worlds. Although he never considered himself a "Filipino American," to many of us who were inspired by his lyrical intellectual musings, NVM was the quintessential Filipino American intellectual. We spent many hours discussing Filipino culture and identity, problems with youth and gangs, and the class divide. Filipinos. All of its problems notwithstanding, NVM gave a kind interpretation of the Filipino American community…but only after I've spent a whole night meditating on his "critique."

The Filipino experience in California is a multiracial one, which has its roots in the 1830 marriage of a Filipino named Domingo Felix and his wife Euphrasia, a Coast Miwok. They were married in Point Reyes and settled at Laird's Landing. Today nearly all the Coast Miwoks are part Filipino, including our dear friend Alex Canillo who performs with the Palabuniyan Kulintang Ensemble.

This multiracial theme continued when the first documented Filipino family under the American colonial regime arrived in the port of San Francisco in 1902. Rufina Clemente Jenkins, a mestiza from Naga, Camarines Sur, of Filipino and Spanish parentage, was accompanied by her six-month-old daughter Francesca. Rufina came as a "war bride." Her husband Frank Jenkins was an African American corporal in the U.S. Army's 9th Cavalry, where he also served as a Spanish interpreter. Because of his Spanish language skills, we discover that Jenkins was also part-Mexican, and at home the Jenkins family spoke Filipino, Spanish, and English. This multiracial theme is alive and well today with many Filipinos, especially with Vangie Buell. Her grandfather was an African American soldier who served in the 1898 Spanish-American War in the Philippines and eventually married a Filipina.

As more Filipinos arrived in large numbers in the 1920's to work in the west coast's agricultural industry, the multiracial theme of Filipino American family formation continued. Filipino women comprised a small number of the immigrants, and many Filipino men married Mexican American and European American women and raised multiracial families. In the 1930's, however, interracial marriage was not looked upon kindly by white society, and in 1933 California passed an anti-miscegenation law that prohibited marriage between whites and Filipinos.

Prior to World War II, west coast Filipinos worked mainly in agriculture, domestic service, and the fish cannery industry. They formed communities and lived along side other Asian American communities in Stockton, San Francisco, Los Angeles, Portland and Seattle. During the Great Depression, Filipinos and Mexicans were blamed for the country's labor problems, and in 1934 an immigration restriction act was passed against Filipinos which effectively shut off large-scale immigration. Some of the East Bay FANHS members were born during the 1930's. They form a "bridge generation" between the pre-1965 and post-1965 Filipino Americans.

After World War II, Hawaii exercised a legal option to increase labor recruitment, and thousands of Filipino immigrants arrived. In the 1960's, many Filipino Americans of this generation—including many East Bay FANHS members—participated in the Civil Rights movement and protested against the Vietnam War. Today the Filipino American community is one of the largest Asian groups in California and continues to grow and evolve. Post-1965 immigrants comprise the majority of Filipino immigrants, and agricultural work is no longer their primary occupation. Because of the changes in the immigration law, preference is given to those with college degrees and professional skills and training. Consequently, many of the stories heard in this collection are about a time and place that no longer exists, and therein lies the value of this book. It is a tribute to the manangs and manongs and the life that they lived.

We have presented these works in public readings and conferences at Chicago, Portland, San Francisco, and Manila. These stories are a labor of love and a way of preserving our family stories for future generations of Filipino Americans and the general public. The editors of this book have done a marvelous job of bringing the project to completion. As these stories will testify, the communities like Alameda, Berkeley, Fremont, Hayward, Oakland, San Francisco, Union City, Livingston, Vallejo, and Stockton provide a rich and multicolored fabric to that experience which we call Filipino American.

SECTION I
What Are You

ROOTS

R. Baylan Megino-Cravagan

9:30 p.m. Finally, we were on our way. As the city slipped into slumber and the crystalline lights faded behind me, I realized that to get on this plane the last thing I had to do was to strip away all my non-essentials – the extra baggage that would not fit on the journey from America to my cultural homeland, the Philippines. As we traveled from the rush of San Francisco to the tropical rest stop in Hawaii, I sank into my seat to travel back in time.

On the plane I read a tiny article about the awarding of "Certificates of Ancestral Domain Claims." A total of 23 CADCs had been given to

1

indigenous tribes for a total of 376,540 hectares, or 930,430 square miles. I wondered if these CADCs were based on anything like American Indian reservations in the U.S. What place and level of respect within society are given to these peoples? I wondered about the peoples in these areas – Kalinga, Puerto Princesa, the Mangyans, Zamboanga del Norte and del Sur, Basilan, Abra, Benguet, Ifugao, Mountain Province, Bohol, Lanao del Norte and del Sur, Nueva Vizcaya, Kasibu, and Quirino. Who determines their value?

I was enjoying a mental flight with the birds and watching the sun spread its orange-pink rays across the horizon, when we broke through the clouds. Mist lay on the mountain lakes and patchwork farmland led up to green hills. As we moved closer to the city areas I saw plots of brown land, a shanty town sprawling next to a cemetery, small homes crowded impossibly close together.

As we landed, men were working in a wide trench, hand digging. We had left the land of high technology and arrived in a country run mostly by manual labor. As we stepped from the plane's controlled atmosphere, the thick Manila air hung around us as though we had walked into a hot steam bath after a dry sauna. Welcome to the Philippines!

Shortly after our arrival, we toured the Rizal monument and Fort Santiago in Intramuros. Throughout our travels, all the people we met were friendly, helpful, happy to talk and to share. I became aware of the respect for and coexistence of what has gone before and what exists now.

Our first major activity was attending the National Theatre Festival (NTF) – only the second of its kind. I found it interesting that the theme of the NTF was "Revolution." What were the artists struggling to keep alive? In one short skit I watched a group handle malong so they became a wall, a house, a vinta, a rotating, floating flower. In another, I saw characters try desperately to communicate without speaking.

As a dancer, I was most affected by the dance drama of the T'boli tribal hero, Tud Bulul. The T'boli dancer executed a lot of fast, continuous little steps, rising and falling, bent at the waist, face stationary, arms and hands flowing. One imagined a hummingbird drinking nectar. Bells hung from women's belts and necklaces. Beads cascaded from earrings and necklaces. Bright colors abounded. A woman created music wherever she went, and could not move without being heard. The drama was breathtaking from beginning to end.

This piece had evolved over two grueling years through the efforts of the leaders of the Kahayag Community Dance and Theatre Group. Tribal research requires going into the mountains, living among the people, and listening to oral stories. This tribal legend was researched, choreographed, performed for the tribe back in the mountains for their feedback, and changed to incorporate their comments. After two years of hard, difficult work with both new and experienced dancers, the group suffered a crushing disappointment when they were not accepted in the first round of NTF auditions. Somehow the festival organizers changed their minds, and the Kahayag dancers had their premier performance in a national venue. Unbelievably, there were no plans for a second performance. Their only steady support was from the local mayor. What is the future of this piece? What is the future of the dance group? After two long years of struggle, will this exquisite performance piece of mythological triumph die? Who would step up to save it? In a largely impoverished country, there is little national interest in supporting the indigenous arts.

The Pintig group from Chicago explored the struggle to define our inner and outer identity. What is it to be a Filipino American? Watching their play, I remembered receiving a slightly uneasy yet encouraging acknowledgment, "You are so ethnic. You like so many Filipino cultural things." So much of Manila reflected the acquired western culture. Do you have to reject the past to move into the future?

Another transition from night to day, waiting in the dingy bus station at midnight, waiting to move to the cool mountain air of Baguio. These are some thoughts on our trip:

♦ Manila's commercial trade items, a smattering of ethnic goods.

♦ In Baguio, I learned about "tawad," Filipino bargaining, and started to sense that point at which mutual benefit quickly slides into the morass of exploitation and greed.

♦ In the mountains, the rich textiles, the lush food, the feel of the earth in all things.

♦ The tranquility of a European park with a lagoon-like body of water. Rowboats on the lake.

♦ Small children sharing secrets across the park bench.

♦ The comfort of academia at the University of the Philippines at Baguio – cloistered, cocooned. They knew nothing, repeat nothing of the Filipino American experience beyond the *balikbayan's* seeming happiness with their lives here. They knew nothing of the struggle to be in a white man's land, the struggle to live, to make a living, to be seen. After the shock of seeing the hotel sign "Absolutely No Filipinos Allowed," a student asked, "If it is so hard there, why don't you come home?" They don't understand.

♦ The open pit mine was like "the Golden Spike" – announcing a new era, change that was the death knell of all that was. Rice terraces became vegetable truck farms for the city. Mining gold, silver and copper for other lands depleted natural resources, never to be replaced or returned.

♦ The Dap-ayan ti Kultura iti Kordilyera (DKK) group, an alliance of cultural workers formed to develop and promote their indigenous art forms that creates theatre pieces incorporating dance, music and songs of the Cordillera. The tribal dances with intricate steps are seldom performed because they are so difficult. Will they be lost to the next generation?

♦ Learning to play various instruments made from bamboo, and marveling at the range in tone and timbre.

♦ The striking Narda weavers saying to the owners, "You can afford a lavish wedding, but you do not pay me enough so I can feed my children." Their stoicism and conviction almost on the verge of – defeat? Resignation? What do they have left?

♦ The Baguio Market building where one whole floor once was filled by antique dealers, now houses only two or three. The mountain tribes have ransomed their heirlooms – the gold alloy gangsa, the huge shell, bead and horn jewelry, the back-strap loom woven cloth, the beaded and feathered headdresses, the intricately woven baskets, the ritual bowls, the burial urns. Most products of traditional handwork were almost extinct. Even the woodcarvers now are making Buddhas and ladies of Thailand with hair coiled high.

How do you pass on a legacy that no longer has much material substance? What is our heritage?

It is seen in the spirit of the artists, in the musicians and the dancers. They protect and preserve and meld the core and soul of the Philippine heritage. For them, dance and music are not performance – they are extensions of life, like fingers on a hand.

Long ago I realized our youth needed a sense of their culture and their roots. Now I know I must teach dance and culture in context. Where is the dance from? What was life like when the dance was created? What is the land like? The climate? What are the issues the people face today? In this way, a bridge is created between the past and the present, between the people in the Philippines and those in America.

The words from the DKK's Salidummay (the name of a group of musicians formed to promote and popularize the indigenous music of the Cordillera) tape have taken on a profound meaning for me. The song is called, "Bebsat San Kaigorotan," (Brothers and Sisters of Kaigorotan).

Brothers and sisters of Kaigorotan
Loved by Kabunian
Since long ago through ancestors

Kabunian gave us culture
To distinguish our races
This is valuable teaching
Do not be ashamed of it or cast it aside.

Teachings and lessons
Modern or ancient
May they not stifle
The handsomest facets of our culture.

If you forget culture
You will lose the images of the ancestors
and forget your place in history.

Our various traditions
in song, dance, and the forging of solidarity
Cooperation and the forging of pacts
Are valuable things in life.

Let us choose in favor of our culture.
Let us honor the ancestors
especially if it is required
By the flow of the times.

Now, comrades
Let us unite
To defend our culture
In the Kaigorotan homeland.

My cultural heritage is deeply rooted in the Philippines. Those roots extend across the vast Pacific Ocean to America. Here, where we struggle to stand and be counted even as we strive to understand and define who and what we are, here is my home. This is where I must be planted and grow.

---

malong, tubular cloth with multiple uses, e.g. sarong, skirt, shawl, shoulder drape, headdress, etc., common to southern Philippines
gangsa, hand-held gong of tribes in northern Philippines
balikbayan, a Filipino visiting the Philippines

BEING PILIPINO

Tony Robles

Being Pilipino
      and black
or black
      and Pilipino
is a chocolate chip cookie

Are you more cookie
or
      more chocolate
chip?

The dark part
      sometimes gets hidden
      on the bottom, but
it sticks to the soul
      and is strong
and you just know
      it's there

And sometimes
      the whole thing
drowns itself
      in milk

and crumbles to
the bottom

Always trying to float
      to the top
      but turns to mush
submerged and
watered down
sweetness and warmth
hidden
         to where you'd never have noticed
           there ever was a cookie

Sweet and warm and
        brown and chocolate black

Pilipino
    and black

   Now that's
   something
   sweet.....

THE MAIL BOX

Gloria Balanon Bucol

The year was 1960 and I was just beginning my junior year at our new high school in Merced, a small rural town in the Central San Joaquin Valley. Previously, I had attended Merced High School but a new high school had been built. The boundaries through the town had been established and since our farm was on the "good" side, I was among the fortunate ones who would get to attend the new high school, El Capitan. My three older sisters and only brother had already graduated from Merced High. Since few Filipino families lived in town during the 1960's, I was the only Pinay to attend El Cap. It was promising to be a grand year – I had been chosen to be editor-in-chief of the school newspaper and my best friend was class secretary.

My family lived outside the city limits on a small fifteen acre farm. My parents had bought the farm in 1940 and they seemed barely able to eke out a living out of those fifteen acres for a family of seven. They farmed tomatoes, bell peppers and later on, went into almond orcharding. You know how some people say they were poor but didn't know it at the time? Well, I wasn't one of those. We were poor and you'd better believe I knew it. How could you not know it when your friends had nice homes, always seemed to have clothes that were in style, and got to be transported home in nine-passenger station wagon car pools while you either had to walk or take the bus?

One early fall morning that year in 1960, I was walking out to the end of our driveway to catch the school bus. My heart sank as I caught sight of my mother by the side of the road, on the other side of the driveway, hammer and shovel in hand, working on our mailbox. Oh, my God! It was almost time for the bus to come and here was my mother, fixing the mailbox. Mama didn't look like my other friends' mothers. I rarely saw her in a dress; she was always in denim work pants, a too-large man's work shirt, and wore a work hat and scarf on her head to protect her skin from the sun. I knew that I would be just humiliated if my school mates saw my mother out by the bus stop fixing our mail box like a regular field hand!

"Mama," I implored her, "please go into the house. Why do you have to fix the mail box now? The bus is coming!" Mama just looked at me and continued digging around the mail box hole. (I think the mailbox was leaning so she was trying to make it stand erect!) Meanwhile, I was becoming frantic. I was desperately trying to ask her to go into the house but at the same time, trying not to sound too disrespectful. *Awan iti baen mo?* Have you no shame? That whole Filipino stigma of shame! Just then, the bus came into view. In the distance, I could see it stop at the Kennedy's, then next door at the McKee's and oh, my God, our's was the next stop! I could feel my body enveloped in a cold sweat as Mom just continued digging the mail box hole, ignoring my respectful pleas, the bus coming closer and closer. I knew then that nothing I could do or say would make her leave and go into the house.

I was resigned to my fate. I was hoping the earth would just open and swallow me. Anything would be better than this humiliation. The bus drew closer and closer, finally stopped right in front of us, its doors swung open, and I hesitantly climbed the steps to enter. As I walked down the aisle, I looked up and saw the kids on the bus, looking curiously at Mom through the windows, then at me to see my reaction. I walked straight ahead, my head high, just thinking—just let any one say anything and I would punch them.

It was not until many years later that I came to understand the significance of this small incident. Now, when I look back, I can only think of what courage it must have taken for my mom to proudly continue fixing the mail box, looking straight into the bus, almost defiantly meeting the stares of my school mates. Certainly she knew she was dressed unlike their mothers, that she looked like a farmer, that she was different, and even spoke with an accent! But the lesson I finally learned was that no matter what your origins, your station in life, and even if you don't quite "fit in," you can still be proud of what you are. You can still be proud even if you're just fixing a mailbox. This, along with my mother's daily modeling of strength, determination, hard work, and a respect for education, my mother taught me to be proud of being myself and being Filipino!

The author's Mom, Alipia Baladad Balanon, member of the Women's Auxiliary of the Legionario del Trabajo, circa 1945.

CULTURAL ENGINEERING

=== *Willie F. Fernandez* ===

I am the son of Juliana and Nicholas Fernandez who came from the town of Binmaley in the province of Pangasinan in the Philippines. I am the second of four children. I was born and raised in the city of Berkeley, where I went through the Berkeley Unified School system.

I earned my bachelor of arts degree in psychology at San Francisco State University. After working as a social worker for five years in Alameda County, I decided to go back to school at the age of 30. I attended the University of California Hastings College of the Law where I earned my juris doctorate.

After deciding not to practice law, I embarked on a career in the human resources field, specializing in affirmative action and employee relations. In 1986, after working in the private and public sectors, I started my own human resources consulting business. In addition to my consulting, I recently accepted a part-time position as the director of an anti-tobacco education project for Filipino youth.

The way I conduct my business is based on the principle of "pluralism." Whether I am conducting a workshop on "diversity", facilitating a strategic planning session, or interacting with the project staff, I try to promote mutual respect, understanding, cooperation and productivity among people who are different. I help people learn how to tear down personal walls and build personal bridges. In short, to become cultural engineers. The name of my business is Cultural Engineering.

My story about my Filipino American experience begins in 1948. You already know the ending - the work that I do today around the principle of pluralism. I believe that an experience I had in 1948 is directly related to why I do my work the way I do.

In 1948, I was in the third grade at Washington Elementary School. Our teacher, one day, decided to teach us about "race." She explained that there were three kinds of races in the world: Negroid, Mongoloid, and Caucasoid. In our class - in our school - there was not a Negroid. You were either Caucasoid or Mongoloid.

She proceeded to go around the class and tell each pupil what category they fit into. But when she got to me, she didn't tell me what category I fit into. Instead, she asked me what I thought I was.

I looked at my friend Richard Sanchez since he had a Spanish sounding name like mine and who she identified as being Caucasoid. I looked at my friend Norman Haraguchi who looked like me and who she identified as being Mongoloid. I was confused. I started to cry. She asked me what she identified Norman as being. I answered, through my tears, "You said he was a Mongoloid." She replied, "Yes, you are a Mongoloid."

From then on I started collecting different labels that I could attach to myself so that I could identify with a group. The only Filipinos I knew, growing up in Berkeley, were my brother and two sisters. I attached many labels to myself in my efforts to "fit in." In 1948 I was Mongoloid, and Malaysian, according to my Uncle Marciano. In the 1950's I was Mexican, Negro, Chinese and Japanese. Later I was an Asian. I was also a WMCLP, a white middle class liberal professional.

I was never comfortable with these labels, with fitting in. But I was very comfortable working with groups of people as a facilitator and trainer. I learned to use a training process that I call "MeTheeWe." This is a process based on a foundation of respect: respect for self (Me), respect for others (Thee) and respect for the social system (We) that the individuals are part of.

Facilitating is my way of managing the inner conflict I have about labels. Being a member of the East Bay Chapter of the Filipino American National Historical Society does not provide me with the label of "Filipino." On the contrary, it provides me with a feeling of "oneness." I feel the connectedness through the sharing of our different Filipino American experiences. We do not see our differences as problems. We see them as resources.

There is a strong connection between what happened to me in the third grade and why I do my work the way I do. To quote Martin Luther King Jr. "We may have all come on different ships, but we're in the same boat now."

UNCLE'S TOP

Herb Jamero

A top so unlike that of the bright, shiny tops bought in town that I felt ashamed even as I was telling Uncle Doloy what a great top he was making just for me. When I had come home earlier that day from school, he asked what I was so sad about. I just had to tell him about the spinning tops the other kids had and how much fun they were all having. And me, sneaking looks at them and wishing that I could have one the same as they. I just knew I couldn't have one. "How lucky they are," I sighed feeling left out and different. It just seemed so unfair.

The next day my uncle said he had a surprise for me. "See, this is the way we make tops back home," he said proudly while carving a top from a block of a hardwood tree. Chips fell at his feet as he took his carving knife to the block of wood. I tried to tell him that I wanted a top from a store just like the others but I couldn't say it. However, I couldn't help but notice the sure way his knotted hands were cutting into the wood as if he could see what was in it and thus make something. When he finished, it looked like a top but not really. It wasn't smooth or rounded. It wasn't even shiny! At the tip was a nail. And, it was wound by a brown, heavy string that looked like a rope! Not the white tightly curled string that came from the store.

I think I said "Thank you" in a way intended to hide my disappointment but he seemed to sense something was not quite right. However, he didn't say anything. Instead, he just showed me how to wind the top and throw it in a funny, side armed motion rather than straight over the top. It spun, but it seemed so big and bulky.

The rest of the week I hid it at home and just watched the other kids with their store bought tops. When I got home I would take it from its hiding place and wished it were like all the others. Once in a while I would practice the way my uncle did. It felt and looked so strange but yet it would spin in its own slow deliberate way. Sometimes Uncle would see me and encourage me to keep practicing.

In the meantime, the kids kept teasing me since I did not have a top - until one day I yelled out, "I do, too!"

"Then where is it?" they chorused.

"I'll bring it tomorrow, you'll see!"

Afterwards, I couldn't believe what I said. Me? Bring my homemade top to school and have everyone laugh! I wished I could take those words back! But it was too late.

The next morning I took the top from its hiding place and put it in my lunch bag to take to school. All morning kids kept coming to me and asked if I was playing against them for a game of "keeps" at lunchtime. "Sure am," I said in a voice that had more conviction than I actually felt. I wasn't ready. I just wanted to be home. Why couldn't I just have kept quiet. Wasn't it bad enough that I was different without having a top different too?

At lunch, everyone rushed to the play yard and I slowly made my way to a smaller group where tops were being spun. In this particular game of "keeps" the object was to hit the other tops while spinning and to knock it off its spin while yours kept spinning. If you did this, then you won the game and could keep the top if you chose.

When at last it was my turn and the kids saw what I had they laughed and shouted "That won't even spin!" But I knew it would and could spin very well even though not in a pretty, whirling blur. Imagine our shock and surprise when my top could not be knocked down. Somehow, it managed to have enough strength to keep spinning while their's wobbled, tumbled and fell. The same was true when I hit their tops and they went hurtling away after being hit by mine. Of course, each time I threw, it was with greater and greater confidence. By this time, all the kids were looking and watching with wonder, "How was this happening?"

When the bell rang to tell us it was the end of the lunch hour, I was the lunch champion. Everyone was saying "Nice going," and asking about my top. All I could say was this was a special top made by my uncle just for me and I had the only one like it in the whole, wide world. How true this was! How could I know that such a top could never be copied.

All the way home on the bus, I was feeling so happy and proud not only for my funny looking top but for my uncle who only wanted me to be happy. As soon as my uncle came home from working in the fields I rushed over to him and gave him a big hug. I didn't care about his dusty, dirty, and sweaty work clothes. He only looked at me with a knowing smile, ruffled my head and didn't say a word.

Not until many years later did I learn this was a game along with the yo-yo that was very popular in the rural areas of the Philippine Islands, the ancestral land of my parents and uncle. Many Filipinos like my uncle were very good at these games. This incident helped me become more aware of my culture and heritage as well as teaching me the value of how something made with care and personal attention is worth more than anything that can be bought.

Herb Jamero in Livingston, CA, 1995

NOT WANTED

Herb Jamero

" GO AWAY ! "
" YOUR KIND NOT WANTED ! "
Words and sounds said harshly and
        with hate.

How come ?
What did I do ?
Is this what happens to those who
        merely seek their fate ?

No !
Not so !
My heart, my mind fighting back
        my tears.

I go !
I find !
To be safe, protected from my fears.

But wait !
Is this what I want ?
To leave the Islands only to live in
        an island ?

I fight !
I stay !
And make this place my land !

WHAT ARE YOU?
GROWING UP FILIPINA IN THE U.S.A.

=== *Trudy Bonzo Chastain* ===

I remember it like it was yesterday, one of my best friend's mothers asking me, "What are you?" I was 11. I ran home to Mama. "Mama, Mrs. Longaberger wants to know, what am I?" "Tell her," said Mama, Blanche Irene Georgia Bonzo, "You're part Mama and part Daddy!" "And," she continued, "You are mestiza." The year was 1952.

That was, really, the first overt question about my race. I was an anomaly, to myself, anyway, because our father, the Filipino part of me, no longer lived with us. Rumors flew as we moved from San Francisco to Kansas, Nebraska, and finally to Stockton, California. Were we adopted?

Why did we have a white mother? What was the deal? The deal was my parents met at the University of Nebraska where daddy (Hipolito Nagal Bonza, aka Jerry) was studying agriculture and Mama was teaching - not at the University but near there. I'm the youngest of five children and I write what I remember hearing of family history before I was born or could remember.

Most of my real memories began in Stockton where we came after two years in Nebraska, where I attended kindergarten and first grade. To me, arriving in Stockton was like coming home. There were familiar people – people we had known in the P.I. - familiar social get-togethers that seemed to always include food, which was fine with me, and a sense of community. I think, really, some of the happiest years of my life were spent in Stockton. True, we lived in a housing project, had no car, not much money but there was plenty to eat and always something going on.

Let me begin, then, in 1947 when we arrived there from Nebraska. We stayed upstairs at Trinity Presbyterian Church (when it was still downtown), presided over at that time by Reverend and Mrs. Legare. Now, I never thought twice about the fact that Rev. Legare was Filipino and Mrs. Legare was white. That was like my parents! I did, however, marvel at the fact that they had a son, Maurice, after finding out the "facts of life." I must mean, my little mind said to itself, that they do that too! What a revelation! I didn't think badly of them, just marveled that people so revered would do such a human thing.

But back to our living places. I was extremely attached to my mother and must have moved more times than anyone can remember during the war years in the Philippines plus in two years had been in three states.

So…one of my main memories is of being held back, screaming and crying, while my mother went somewhere. I thought she might not come back. My father hadn't, nor had my brother, Billy, who died during the war at age 10 in 1943. I survived. Mama came back. Then on to our temporary domicile in a railroad car which had been made into a "home." Finally, we settled in a house on Clay St. (I think), and I attended second grade at Jackson School.

In the summer of 1948, we moved to River View, the housing project out by Lewis Park. No longer there, except in my mind's eye. I can see the courtyard where we lived, three long buildings of four units each. Ours was Number 13C. Brown industrial type linoleum, kerosene heating, an actual ice box with the drip pan you had to empty each night or wake up to a mini-flood in the morning. But to me it was heaven. There were grass, marigolds and hollyhocks which Cecil planted, trees, kids to play with, swings and "monkey bars." Who could ask for anything more? Cecile even planted a vegetable garden and I could have one of my favorite treats, green onion sandwiches – made with white bread and mayonnaise. I still like them. So many memories crowd in now: the laundromat with the frontloading Bendix machines, the clothesline where I tried to chin myself with John Henry's help (a neighbor boy) and ended up chipping a tooth when he dropped me. The ice plant and the way it smelled tangy – when we played hide and go seek. I was very happy there and wish we could've stayed longer than we did. Eventually, of course, it was closed and torn down being, after all, temporary war housing.

Slowly, however, the older siblings moved out. Mary to go to nursing school and then to U.C. Berkeley; Cecil to get married to Betty Acoba;

Patty to go to Quaker Boarding School, Scattergood, where I also went later, in Iowa. By the time I was 11 it was just Mama and me and we had to move out of our three bedroom unit to the "cracker boxes," #126. These were more compact but still nice in my eyes. I made new friends but still I could see my old ones. Life went on. Cecil came and got us for special occasions at the Acobas or church and I was quite content. Actually, I was told later I was a "spoiled brat" but then no one's perfect.

The bubble burst in 1953, during the McCarthy era. Because sister Mary went to a peace conference in China she was labeled a communist by the Stockton Record and the school district stopped calling Mama for her substitute teaching. We had no money. We had to move. I went for the summer - a very happy summer - to Van Nuys in Southern California with my Aunt Joyce and Uncle Dave. Mama - and Mitzi, our long-haired kitty - went to Berkeley to stay with newlyweds Mary and Lou. Double trouble: Mary and Lou were allergic to cats and Mitzi's hair got all over Lou's silkscreens! But it was only for the summer.

That fall, Mom and I were reunited in Leggett, a small logging town about 100 miles south of Eureka. She landed a good paying full-time job away from the House UnAmerican Activities Committee hearings in San Francisco. I, however, did not fare well. I was the only "person of color" there, was away from my extended family and childhood friends, and I entered puberty. A crucial time. We had no car (never had in my memory – but there were always city buses or rides from friends), no phone, just a little summer cottage to live in. I became extremely depressed and Mama called Mary to come get me. I was a little happier at James Lick Junior High in San Francisco but really sort of hibernated until I reached

Scattergood.

Scattergood. Imagine gentle, green rolling hills, extreme quiet, twelve acres of beautiful but simple school grounds with a main building built in 1890. That was the Scattergood I came to in 1954 and left, so much enriched in 1958. I did everything from canning tomatoes to milking cows to raising a prize-winning barrow (neutered male pig) for a 4-H project.

I was accepted to the University of California at Berkeley and began there in the fall of '58. Berkeley, what a shock to go from a student body of 50 at Scattergood to one of 20,000! My first semester was very challenging but I didn't sink, I swam. I changed my major from social work to German (which for some reason I excelled in, coming in third in Iowa in a high school test) and staying on that course, intending to become a German teacher, until my interest began to wane. I dropped out of school after two and a half years to reconsider my major and changed my life's course by marrying my college sweetheart, Charles Chastain, and having our wonderful sons, Michael and John (born Oct. '62 and Oct. '63 respectively). I later returned to my studies at a junior college, earning a state child care certificate and taking many courses for self-interest and improvement including the history of Asians in the United States. What an eye opener that was. I had no idea how discriminated against we had been: actually legislated against, barred from social gathering places, signs reading "No dogs or Filipinos Allowed," burned out, even killed. No wonder I didn't feel so good about the Filipina part of my heritage.

Now, however, the pendulum has swung the other way and perhaps whites feel excluded from our gatherings and maybe jealous of our wonderful "ethnic" ways of cooking, celebrating and BEING. I now revel in having a Filipino heritage in this day and age and even feel stronger for having survived the economic and other hardships our family endured. Previous generations had it even harder here in the States. What is important to remember, I think, is that we are all basically members of the same race, the human race. I remember explaining to one of our sons for about 45 minutes one afternoon when he was around eleven and cavorting on the front lawn doing somersaults and such that he should be proud of his Filipino heritage. He listened and finally said, "Do you want to know what I think?" "Yes," I answered. "I don't think it matters," he said. In a way, he's right. But in another way, we need to keep gathering, keep teaching, keep celebrating and keep recording our histories – so that nothing is lost and all can be woven into an on-going tapestry of living Filipino(a) in the good old U.S. of A.

---

mestiza or mestizo, a person of mixed racial heritage

**The family of Hipolito (Jerry) Nagal Bonzo and Blanch Georgia
Bonzo. The author is the youngest in the center. 1941.**

I USED TO HEAR GRANDMA

Tony Robles

I used to hear Grandma
   talk on the phone
      in Tagalog
     in the front room
       on the couch
And it was in those moments
   when she seemed
      to be the happiest

Laughter rang
   across the ocean
      over the rooftop
       in the attic
through the pot of adobo
      and under the pot of rice
      over that beige rotary telephone

And her voice became music
   in those moments
      she was no longer Ma,
     or Grandma,
      or Mrs. Robles
Just herself
    happy
      and naked to the sky

Although I didn't understand Tagalog
     I felt its beauty in my Lola's voice
I saw the sun rise

in the front room
every time she spoke
what was in her heart

Used to wonder
who was on the other line
whoever it was
they knew us
knew if we did good in school
if we like to eat *bibingka*
if we were *pogey* or *pangit*
Even knew if we were wearing
clean or dirty drawers

The phone would ring
and the music would start
in the front room
with my Lola

My dad and uncles
would be in the back
drinking Ripple
and singing songs

My Girl
and Smokey
Oooh, Baby, Baby
and the Temptations
and the Impressions...all the old heavies

And that....was cool

It melted into us like pomade
melting on our gas stove

34

It was in our blood
      and we drank it down
      and passed it all around

But the music
  from my Lola
when the phone rang
  told us
that the sun
  did indeed set
in Lola's room
  and rose
to the sound
  of her
  voice

---

pogey (pogi), handsome
pangit, ugly
bibingka, rice cake

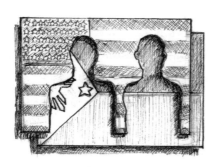

TWO BROTHERS: *Two Filipino American Perspectives*

James Sobredo

As a Filipino American in the 1980s and 1990s, I shall always remember Reaganomics and the "Decade of Greed." Under the Reagan administration, I saw financial aid programs and scholarships for racial and ethnic minority groups dwindle and in some cases disappear all together. I did not approve of Reagan's policies, so through it all, I was always attending demonstrations against the Reagan-Bush policies. In the 1990s, my political activism continued: I was protesting with thousands of people in San Francisco against American military actions in the Persian Gulf War.

The majority of my undergraduate Filipino friends were not like me. They were more conservative, and after college they became successful engineers, accountants, and health professionals. My Filipino friends had a fairly smooth and successful transition to the privileged professional, middle class, and they fit the media's image of Asians as "model minorities"—that is, people who worked hard, sacrificed, and, in spite of a history of racial discrimination, persevered and succeeded. Upon examination, I too seem to fit this model minority category: my family came to America as poor immigrants from the Philippines and eventually worked their way into the middle class. My father worked as a mechanic for the Navy, my mother a middle school teacher. Their son went on to attend one of the top doctoral programs in the country and received a prestigious fellowship.

Filipino Americans like me and the rest of my college-educated Filipino friends receive all the media's attention. We are the stuff that myths, like the model minority construction, are made of.

Before coming to Berkeley I was attending an Ivy league university. My younger brother Johann was pumping gas at a gas station, which caused for me, to put it mildly, a bit of "psychic disequilibrium." Johann would be dodging the local police who had a warrant out for his arrest for having outstanding tickets for illegal drag-strip racing. He was the undefeated local drag-strip champion in the quarter-mile. Johann hung out with 15 other teenagers, his buddies (his *barkada*), who formed an informal racing group called the "Eliminators." Outsiders, the media, for example, who didn't know any better, would call the Eliminators a "gang." And it's true that individual members of the Eliminators sold drugs, got involved in fights, and some were even involved in "drive-by" shootings. The crucial term here is "individual members" for they never did any of these acts as a group. In a word, they were not really a gang for they did not defend turf; they did not extort money; they had no formal initiation rites; and they had no formal gang leader who issued orders— although my brother was a sort of informal leader of the group. Fortunately, my brother never dealt drugs, never started fights or shot anyone. The Eliminators were simply a bunch of restless young men who hung out together and didn't know what they wanted in life.

The reality of the matter is, although we both came from the same family, my brother's experience in our family differs greatly from mine. I was born in the Philippines, and when my family came to America, we were very poor. So I understood how difficult life was, and consequently worked very hard to make sure that I don't stay poor and non-privileged for the rest of my life.

My younger brother, on the other hand, never experienced hardship while he was growing up, and by the time he was a senior in high school, he had his own new car complements of my parents. Then, the following year Reagan's decade of greed began. My mother went on strike, and, like the striking airport traffic controllers, whom Reagan fired, she too was fired from her job. At the same time, my father had a stroke and had to quit his job. Hence, during the decade of greed in which the rich got richer, my family dropped out of their middle-class status.

Disillusionment quickly got the better of my brother when he realized that there would be no money for him to attend college and his period of restless searching started. I taught Asian American studies at U.C.-

Berkeley, and I listened to lots of Filipinos talk about their experiences and also those of their friends. Their stories were similar to my Johann's. Like many young Filipinos who have no direction and consequently no hope for the future, Johann turned to hanging out with his *barkada* who were just as lost as he was.* Unfortunately, as a result of this hanging out with friends, a lot of Filipinos get into trouble, for example, with gangs, the police, drugs, and alcohol.

My brother was one of the lucky ones. On his own volition, he left the Eliminators and now works as a supervisor for Northwest Cargo. He still hasn't figured out what exactly he wants to do with his life, but at least he's planning on returning to college and getting a degree.

Thus, while the education route worked for me because my family could afford to send me to college, in the Reaganomics of the 1980s, however, it was not an option that was available to my brother. Striking workers are fired from their jobs, and scholarship funds and programs were eliminated. My brother's experience shows the reality behind the myth of the "model minority."

Postscript: Johann is currently a successful manager of an international air-freight company. He and his wife, Wendy, and their daughter, Angelina, live in Saipan.

---

barkada, a social group of close friends, gang.

*N.b. there is no comma after "Filipinos," so this is a restrictive clause, which means I am talking about Filipinos "who have no direction". This is not to say that all Filipino youth have no direction, or that they all get into trouble.

HANDFULS OF RICE

Tony Robles

The old man's hands
      were rough and brown
marked and lined and callused
cupped to conceal
a cracked frown
with unsaid words
      he ate
one handful of rice
      at a time

I say *handful*
      not that he didn't use a fork
      he'd used forks
and was quite intimate with a knife
      but that's another story

His mock disgust towards me dripped
      from thick brown fingertips
as he scooped another handful of rice
      and tuna fish
and raised it to his shiny lips

"Hmmm…you take after your mother
      you're two of a kind
      you better stick with potatoes
I'm one-fourth Irish on my mother's side

He would grab a piece of squid
    in its blackness
and drop it
    in his mouth
and growl at me and laugh

You don't know what's good
I'd eat something made special for me
    a pork chop
    or hamburger
And the old man would see
    the future again
one handful of rice at a time

And one day after listening
to how I was more potatoes than rice
    more Irish than Pinoy
 I closed my eyes
    and put the squid in my mouth
    it had been in a pot
black with bay leaves floating atop

And I tasted what my father felt
    the black ink of the squid was
on my hands
    and traveled through my veins
and settled in my heart

I felt like I was born in that black pot of squid

And the old man just looked at me
in mock disgust
and went back to his rice
one handful
at a time

MAEDA'S PLACE

Peter M. Jamero

Our follow-the-crops migration ended about the time I was ready to start the first grade in 1936. Papa found a place in Livingston owned by a Japanese farmer named Yoshitaro Maeda. The property was part of the Yamato Colony, the only planned Japanese settlement in U.S. history. The Colony was a series of farms on 3000 acres located on the northeastern boundary of Livingston. The Yamato Colony was laid out in neat rectangular plots of largely grape and peach orchards which continue to be farmed today by descendants of these Japanese pioneers. Maeda was one of the first handful of farmer colonists. His property, one of the largest, was in the middle of the Colony.

The property on which we lived was the original Maeda homestead and consisted of a two bedroom house for the family, a tankhouse, several outbuildings, and a small grove of eucalyptus trees. It was located about two miles from the town of Livingston and connected to the main road by about five hundred feet of dirt road. The property was in the midst of a vineyard of Red Malaga, a popular wine grape of the times. The place was ideal for the family and the ever growing number of Filipino farm laborers who were our extended family. The main house had a long room which was converted into the camp mess hall. The tankhouse was a three level structure typical of the times, with two levels of living space, replete with an Aermotor windmill which provided the power to pump our drinking water. The top level contained a large water tank which occasionally served as a secret swimming pool for Herb and me. The outbuildings were readily adaptable for a bunkhouse and a community bath. And, perhaps just as important, there was plenty of room for the game chickens that were also a standard part of our entourage.

The location was also perfect for Papa's labor contracting business. Earlier, when we lived in Atwater, Papa made a good initial impression on area farmers and growers for the quality of workers he was able to supply during harvest. Maeda's place offered an ideal base from which to build his contracting business. Papa negotiated a rental agreement in which he would provide for all of Maeda's farm labor needs and would maintain the immediate living area. To my knowledge, no cash was included in the rental agreement. We were to stay at Maeda's place for eight eventful years.

These early years of my life were during the Great Depression, a time when few people had jobs, banks literally went bankrupt, homes were lost, and food was in scarce supply. However, this description of the Depression was what I was to learn much later, during my college years. My personal reality at the time was much different. For me, this was a time of frolicking around the countryside of Livingston and in enjoying life…like any other kid. There were many things to keep me occupied. I learned how to make paper airplanes. Out of old newspapers, I fashioned hats and boats that I would sail in the nearby irrigation ditches. From discarded thread spools, rubber bands, and matchsticks I put together a fleet of different size tractors. The men often gave me colorful kites they made out of bamboo and paper, pasted on by day old steamed rice. They also made tops and yo-yo's that were far better than the store-bought. I didn't know at the time that these toys were native to the Philippines. No wonder they spun so well.

I didn't consider ourselves poor. As far as I was concerned we were like most other people we knew at the time. We always had a roof over our heads. Being in the country, we didn't need money in order to eat. We hunted cottontail rabbits and game birds, fished in nearby streams and rivers and picked wild mustard and watercress for salad. We raised and slaughtered our own pigs and chickens. We grew our own vegetables such as tomatoes, *tambaliog* (Chinese squash), eggplant, and stringbeans. When times were really tough, there was always rice and soy sauce and, the ever present *mungus* (mung beans. the source of bean sprouts).

The Depression years were also times when we didn't have electricity or indoor toilets. Papa cooked on a wood stove. Mama did the laundry on a washboard, and those of us kids who could reach the clotheslines hung the wash out to dry. We did our homework by kerosene lamp. The best lights, however, were reserved for the gaming tables that the men hovered over for hours in the evening. The lights were so bright that all kinds of bugs and insects were attracted to them. I often watched with fascination as the insects flew towards the bright light to their certain death.

As for toilets, the old reliable outhouse served our purpose. Except in our case the outhouse was multi-seated to accommodate our growing extended family of farm workers. The only trouble with the multi-seated outhouse was that it was not made for little boys. One hot summer day, Herb nodded off as he was sitting in the outhouse and fell in the pit. A rope was thrown to a grateful but foul smelling Herb. The rope and Herb's clothes were immediately disposed of. As for Herb, he was hosed down and then endured several days in which no one wanted to be near him because of the unbearable stench that just wouldn't go away. The outhouse was also not made for the hens and chicks that freely roamed the camp. Those that were unlucky enough to fall in were pulled out after lowering a pail by rope, enticed to enter the pail by chicken feed.

We did have a nice car. It was a green 1926 Dodge Brothers sedan with a running board and fenders large enough to lay on. Actually, we didn't own it by ourselves. As was the common practice of the time, the car was totally owned by several of my uncles. I don't know what arrangements may have been agreed to by the car's owners. But Papa seemed to have the car most of the time and drove it whenever he wanted.

The Great Depression had little impact on me at the time. I didn't feel deprived. Which is not to say that it did not affect me at all. I now know why we were raised to eat anything that was served, to finish everything on the plate, and to go barefoot most of the time. While I now wear shoes, I still continue to eat whatever is served and finish whatever is put on my plate. Speaking of shoes, we were limited to one pair of good shoes a year, for school. If the shoes wore out, Mama simply inserted a piece of cardboard in the shoe. If I outgrew the shoes, I would somehow squeeze them on for school and took them off as soon as I got home.

Mama did her shopping for us in the Montgomery Ward catalog. I remember looking at the latest fashions for boys but also knowing the clothing would not be for me. Mama was much more practical and frugal in what she ordered. The clothes had to serve our needs for school and for the house which meant they were usually overalls made of durable denim. These were the days before consumer protections so that sometimes what was advertised was not what we received. Thus, some shoes wore out more quickly and sometimes our clothes were the wrong size. The Montgomery Ward catalog also served a number of other purposes. It was one of the few pieces of reading material available to us, a rich source of information to the outside world. And since these were the days before affordable toilet paper, it also served as the main material for reading and other purposes in the outhouse.

※　　※　　※

Looking back at those years, my perceptions were undoubtedly shaped by the limited contact I had with the outside world. Virtually all of my contacts were with people who were like ourselves, Filipino. On those rare occasions when I would be in a town, I looked in wonder at the strange aliens who were white, much taller, had long noses, and spoke a strange language. As a pre-schooler my world was Filipino, everyone else was a foreigner.

My language was in the Visayan dialect of Cebuano, the dialect of persons coming from the islands of Bohol, Cebu, Siquijor, and the southern parts of Negros and Leyte. By this time our extended family had grown from the uncles from Bohol to include these other "uncles". Since "Bisaya" was my only language I was quite fluent and spoke with the Manongs like a native. The Manongs spent a lot of their time talking about the Philippines which was a rich source of my learning about my heritage, culture, and folklore. Their stories were particularly vivid during the outdoor gatherings around the fire that were held on numerous starlit nights. They spoke not only about their memories about the Philippines, but also their dreams, their lives, and hard work here in America. They also spoke about their sexual adventures and misadventures. I listened and learned.

It was probably inevitable that under these circumstances, I became an imaginative story teller. I took many liberties with events I heard from the Manongs. I inserted myself in the middle of most of my made up stories. It didn't matter that I factually mixed up events or that I confused happenings in the Philippines with America or vice versa. I found the men to be a ready and willing audience. I didn't realize it at the time but I believe the reason they were such a great audience was because listening to this little boy talk to them in their native tongue was the next best thing to being back in the Philippines. Since most of the Filipinos of that time were single males, there were only a few families with young children. I was one of the few kids with whom the men had an opportunity to interrelate. In me, these homesick Manongs had someone to connect with here in America besides themselves.

As a boy with a very large imagination, I didn't always understand that my stories shouldn't be told in mixed company, especially in front of Mama. There were many times when Mama gently told me that it was not nice to talk about sexual exploits of the men who were mostly single, young men in their twenties and thirties. She said it was not good to talk about my imagined social adventures with pretty *dalagas* (single young women) even though my stories were highly entertaining to the Manongs. She scolded the men for putting such ideas in my head. This really didn't seem to influence their behavior.

Once, when I was about six years old, one of my "uncles" brought me to a burlesque show in Stockton. I was fascinated by the bumping and grinding and the writhing of the blonde strippers to syncopated swing music. It was also my first glimpse of what women looked like without clothes. The first thing I did when I got home was to show everyone how the stripteasers took off their clothes. Mama was not pleased and proceeded to again scold the now giggling men for exposing me to some of life's realities.

米　米　米

This idyllic lifestyle abruptly came to an end in September 1936 when I started school. Suddenly I was confronted with people talking in

English. Mama tried to prepare me by having me memorize three things in English: my name, my date of birth, and my parents names. This was the extent of my English for virtually the whole first grade. No one understood anything else I said. There were two other Filipino boys in the class but while they understood me, they spoke only English. I was frustrated and felt so alone. This first year of school was probably the only time in my life I've been so quiet.

My lack of English also led to my getting lost on the first day of school. Papa and Mama drove me to school and pointed to the bus I was to take home after class ended for the day. What they didn't realize was that particular bus did not go down our road. After boarding the bus, it didn't take long for me to realize that I was lost. One by one all the children got off the bus. Except me. I tried to explain to the bus driver that he needed to go to the other side of town. He had no idea of what I was trying to tell him. It was now dusk and the sun was low in the west. Suddenly, I saw the familiar house of Hildo Pomicpic, a good friend of Papa's, and signaled to the bus driver to let me off. Manong Hildo drove me home. As we approached the house, I could see Papa waiting for us. I was so happy to see him and to be getting home. Papa's greeting was to take out his belt and whack me on the bottom, at the same time admonishing me for worrying everyone by getting lost.

After my traumatic first day of school, Mama became seriously concerned about my inability to speak English. When I was a toddler, there was an ongoing debate between Papa and Mama regarding what language to teach their first born. Papa insisted that I be taught the traditional Bisaya dialect of Cebuano. As a school teacher, Mama felt that I should be taught the language of their new country. Reluctantly, Mama gave in. Speaking only in the Cebuano dialect did not pose much of a problem in my pre-school years. But after my first day trauma, she was convinced that her eldest child must be taught English. For the remainder of that first year, I underwent a rigorous home course in English, taught by that former Garcia-Hernandez school teacher, my mother.

Mama was innovative in her teaching of English. We started with names of animals and familiar items which she would describe to me in Cebuano. She then pointed to drawings that she made on cardboard obtained from the men's dry cleaned dress shirts, depicting these same animals and articles. She than gave the English equivalent to me to memorize. After teaching me other everyday nouns, we advanced to verbs, adjectives, adverbs, and conjunctions. I was a quick learner. I began to better understand what my first grade teacher, Mrs. Sheesley, was trying to teach us. And, I began to figure out what my classmates were saying. With all this progress, however, I still was not confident of speaking much in school. Apparently, my infrequent verbal contributions in class did not hurt me. At the end of the year Mrs. Sheesley gave me my report card with the notation, "Promoted to the 2nd Grade". I was so proud and happy. So was Mama.

Because Mama was busy in helping operate the camp and taking care of her growing family, my English lessons were conducted at night, by kerosene lamp. So you might say that I have something in common with Abraham Lincoln. We both learned to read and write by kerosene lamp.

I was the only one of the Jamero children whose first language was not English. Papa and Mama learned their lesson in their new country.

The other kids grew up with English. Mama talked to us in English. Papa usually talked to us in Cebuano but we answered in English. I always believed that this method in our communication also led to Papa becoming much more proficient with English. At any rate Papa developed an increasing comfortableness in talking with *puti* (whites).

English was not my only new acculturation experience. I had to learn how to eat *puti* food. On my first day of school Mama fixed my usual lunch of fish and rice which she packed in my brand new metal lunch box. Needless to say, I brought sandwiches thereafter, even though they were wrapped in Langendorf bread paper rather than store bought wax paper like the other kids had.

※　　※　　※

The labor contracting business had grown to such an extent that both Papa and Mama had to work long hours to sustain it. During the peak harvests for peaches and grapes, the camp population swelled to more than eighty. To handle the overflow, some men set up their cots on the front porch. Others were housed in tents. Neither Papa nor Mama had enough time to spend with the children. The older ones were left to their own devices.

This was all right with me because there was so much in my young life when I could occupy myself. I took care of my personal needs and ate alongside the men in the camp mess hall. The outdoors was my playground. It must have been more difficult for Pula and George since they were both so young. On the other hand, there was always a few of our uncles to help out.

One such uncle was called Opong. His given name was Crispo Paguican, also from Garcia-Hernandez, Bohol. He was a second cousin of Papa and was part of the family camp entourage as long as I could remember. He was muscular, well proportioned, and stood four feet seven. Because of his diminutive height, Opong was the butt of unkind jokes and comments. Children would regularly use his height to compare their growth. And probably because his height inspired little respect, most called him by his first name. Even the Jamero children who were brought up to call elders by Manong or Uncle, called him Opong. He was the main child care giver of all the men. He was obedient to a fault. Many of the unpopular tasks he was asked to do by Mama and Papa, such as change diapers, he carried out with rarely a complaint. Opong had a good singing voice and often sang to the little Jameros. And when he was in a particularly good mood he would entertain the whole camp around the evening fire. Unforgettable was the tune in which he would sing the lyrics in three languages — English, Spanish, and Cebuano.

※　　※　　※

The Jamero camp always seemed to be the center of celebrations. Every new baby was given a baptism party complete with *lechon, adobo*, and all the trimmings. Mama was often asked to be godmother to other Filipino kids and since our place already had the necessary cooking facilities, it was held there. We also celebrated the end of various harvests with a big party. The men didn't need much of a reason to celebrate. After all they were still young and single.

The celebrations were always accompanied by music. Many of the men played instruments that they learned to play in the Philippines. They played the guitar, mandolin, *banduria* (a Filipino adaptation of the mandolin), and a washtub bass. Sometimes there would be music from a tenor saxophone or trumpet. They seemed to know all the latest tunes and someone usually had a songsheet or songbook so that everyone could join in. If one of us children would sing, the men would show their appreciation by tossing money on the floor. Sometimes this could amount to a goodly sum so I could always be persuaded to sing. One year I made so much money that I decided to buy Mama a new dress. She was so pleased. As I think back to my singing years I was always able to remember the lyrics, something that I found difficult to do in my adult life.

We all celebrated Christmas and New Years with the same party like atmosphere. The Christmas tree was decorated with different colored paper rings attached to one another. Some years we were able to decorate with store bought snow and silvery paper streamers. Even though the tree had no lights, I always marveled at how beautiful it appeared in the mix of moonlight and kerosene lamp.

With all the camp celebrations, one would think we would celebrate birthdays with cake and presents. But we didn't. Celebrating birthdays was not a Filipino tradition. Filipinos celebrated town fiestas, family reunions, and religious feast days, but not birthdays. My first ever birthday was celebrated when I was already married. Most of the kids we knew had birthday parties, but not the Jamero kids. We were never told why Mama and Papa chose to exclude birthday celebrations.

Two unforgettable events occurred toward the end of our years at

Maeda's place. One evening while eating dinner with the men, we smelled the distinctive odor of burning feathers. We rushed outside to find the chicken coops housing the game hens and the rooster pens burning out of control. Cockfighting has long been a passion for Filipinos. Losing the game chickens was a major loss. A few hours later we learned that the fire was purposefully set by Junior and Pula. Their reason? They felt the men paid more attention to the chickens than to them. Their punishment? Whacks from Papa's belt.

The other event was the beginning of World War II. We were having dinner when a bulletin on the radio announced that Pearl Harbor was bombed. Of more significance to the camp, was that Manila was also under heavy bombardment. The War had the effect of suddenly transforming the image of Filipinos from despised "brown monkeys" to "brave brown brothers". Almost overnight, Filipinos became desirable residents in America. The Filipino response was mixed. Most took a patriotic but somewhat guarded view of the change in the attitude toward them. After all, the overnight change could not completely erase the years of discriminatory treatment they had experienced in America. Some enlisted in the armed forces and went on to serve in the famed 1st and 2nd Filipino Army Regiments. But a few did everything they could to avoid the selective service draft, such as falsely claiming they could not speak or understand English. The war years were also a time of full employment. Not only were the men needed in agriculture but many Filipinos found jobs in airplane plants and shipyards.

My attitude to World War II was also somewhat mixed. At first, I was caught up in the patriotic fervor of the times and in the ethnic pride of being Filipino. But later on, I did not understand why there were no longer any Japanese kids in our midst. I was in the sixth grade when the war started. I always had many classmates of Japanese ancestry. All of a sudden. they were all gone having been evacuated to what were euphemistically called relocation camps. In later years I learned that these were in reality concentration camps which housed mostly American citizens who happened to be of Japanese ancestry.

Papa's reputation as a farm labor contractor was at an all time high during WWII. Not only was he in demand from the farmers, he was also in demand from Filipino farm workers who knew that Papa could be counted on to get top wages for them. The increased demand for workers now meant that Papa had to make many more recruiting trips to Stockton and other nearby communities. He couldn't just sit back and rest on his reputation. He took me on some of his trips which were always an exciting adventure for me. I watched Papa as he persuaded Filipino men to come to work for him. He seemed to instinctively know how best to appeal to different men.

During the war gasoline was rationed, as well as many other durable goods. The amount of gas that one could buy was determined by stickers distributed by the government labeled "A, B,or C". As a farm labor contractor Papa was deemed to be valuable to the war effort and was awarded the highest rated "C" sticker, which entitled him to purchase almost any amount of gasoline. The "C" sticker was definitely prestigious. And to this eleven year old kid, riding in a car with a "C" sticker made me feel special.

My response to our rationing privileges for food was quite the opposite. Because farm labor was considered to be critical to the war effort, Papa and Mama were authorized to buy in bulk and also had priority in purchasing scarce items such as prime cuts of meat, sugar, and soap. We shopped in Livingston's largest market at the time, Ecclefield's. Since these were the days before shopping carts, I usually went along to help carry the grocery bags. As we left the market, I always felt self conscious and somewhat guilty at the stares we would get from other shoppers who were restricted from buying in the same quality and quantity.

The Jamero camp underwent unprecedented growth as agriculture became critical to the war effort. Our economic situation improved considerably during World War II.

A HOT SUNDAY IN MT. EDEN
Reflections at a farmhouse in the late 1960's on land that is now Chabot College in Hayward, California

Teresita Cataag Bautista

Manong Modest strolled along the wooden planks, his dusty boots thumping slowly with each bow-legged step, as he left the paintless outhouse. The creaky outhouse door had caught my attention moments before as I looked up from my math book in the sweaty 75 degree sun.

As I scanned the horizon, I could see Momma coming from the mansion where she had finished another cleaning job for the elderly Chabots. She was removing the green scarf from her wet head and her tiredness showed in her slow gait. I wondered what would be her renumeration this time. She had already earned a fine mahogany China cabinet...maybe that matching buffet table!

As Manong Modest passed me on his way back to the kitchen of the main farmhouse, his bearded grin seemed to say, "What a relief!"

As I followed Manong Modest's laundry-bleached, grey-green plaid shirt and his drooping, baggy khaki trousers, I caught a glance of my little brother chit-chatting with his one year old kid "Goatie." Chris, who just turned four years old, really loved his weekend pet. He was always eager to visit "Goatie" every Sunday, as the family joined other town mates in the weekly ritual of slaughtering a pig or goat.

This Sunday, no large animal was the victim since Manong Modest told the clan, "Just let me cook the *manok.*"

Manong Modest entered the farmhouse, and the sharp slam of the screen door interrupted my waning concentration once more. My arithmetic homework had become unbearably boring.

Momma had now entered the farmhouse and within seconds, she screamed, "Oy! What's this!!!" The kitchen became a clatter of voices in broken English and Ilocano.

I could no longer keep my heavy eyelids open to finish my homework. I walked on to the porch, up to the screen door, and squinted through the rusty screen to see what was creating such a commotion.

Momma, wide-eyed, was holding a still-feathered chicken over a large, steaming pot, as Uncle Francisco rushed to catch the dripping carcass in a big bucket that was used to soak freshly-picked spinach in the kitchen sink. Puzzled, my eyes darted from person to person. By that time, about six shocked adults were scurrying about, chastizing stunned, but not so sober, Manong Modest. The great pot of chicken stock had become feather soup. Chris' Ninong Mel was muttering "Ay 'Sus Mario Sip," pacing nervously back and forth, a half-smoked cigarette hanging from his lips. The howling voices from the kitchen had attracted the attention of Uncle Mel's two dogs, who had been resting in the shade on the side of the farmhouse. They yapped excitedly at the screen door, nudging me away from the screen so they could get a glimpse of the noisy kitchen.

"Oh well," I thought, "…looks like dinner's not gonna be very soon." My empty stomach brought on visions of a big dish of Neopolitan ice cream, with more chocolate than vanilla or strawberry.

I walked off the porch to join my younger sisters, who couldn't be bothered with all the ruckus. Merlita and Magdalena were busy collecting bees in mason jars filled with a little bit of water. They caught the bees hovering around the ripe blackberries at the fence behind the farmhouse. The girls' giggles kept their play oblivious to the fowl fiasco in the farmhouse kitchen. I stood quietly watching their silly courage as I could hear Momma complaining in Ilocano, while she plucked soggy feathers from Sunday's dinner.

I mused, "Maybe I'll just eat rice for dinner!" as Magdalena and Merlita came running over to show me their captured bugs buzzing furiously to escape.

---

manok, chicken

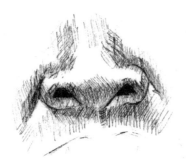

MA! HEY, MA!

Tony Robles

"Ma! Hey, Ma!" Uncle Anthony's voice was a bell as it traveled down the hall. His steps were rhythmic, leaving behind marks of night fights on dirt-covered streets, of loves left behind under moist sheets, and loneliness passed out fully clothed in frustration's weak pulse. Now his voice filled the early morning musty air, occasionally interrupted by the creaking of the carpet covered wooden floor.

"Hey, Ma! Ha, ha. That's my baby girl!"

"Shhh, be quiet, you're so loud, kid!"

"Aw, Ma, you know you're my little Filipino Afro woman with your flat primitive nose."

"You're crazy, kid! Comb your hair! You look like the black guys on the corner."

"Black guys? What you mean black guys, Ma? You ain't got no business talkin' 'bout black guys with your Filipino African nose."

"Shut up, kid," Grandma snapped as Uncle Anthony tried to pinch her nose.

Steam from the hot boiling pot of *sinigang* rose and caressed Grandma's face. The rice boiled wildly in a blackened metal pot.

"You look like a wildman, kid, like from the jungle."

" Aw, Ma, you know how it is."

Ma did know how it is and how it was. She had ten kids, and they had kids, and their kids had kids. But she knew Anthony, her youngest son, and when he needed a haircut.

"Aw, Ma. You cut too much!"

Grandma snapped gently, "You're in America, not Africa. Now be still!"

"Aw, man, Ma. You done messed up my mop!" Locks of shiny black hair sprouted from the floor, some landing on Grandma's fuzzy robe.

"You could stuff a mattress with all this hair," Grandma would say in her Pilipino accent.

Music from Anthony's room filled the halls and his voice covered the pops and scratches echoing from his 45's and 33's. Pictures of Smokey Robinson, Bruce Lee, Muhammad Ali, Joe Louis and African warriors covered the sky-blue walls, punctuated by nails and patched with tape. Sitting in that room was darkness and in the darkness was a light that he shared in his heart.

"Your mop looks good, blood." I had an Afro. "I got something for you, baby boy." He pulled out a handful of hairnets. They were thick, the kind that foodhandlers wore. "That'll keep your mop in place." Uncle Anthony had worked at Children's Hospital in San Francisco and would help himself to the inventory. In fact, Grandma's house was always stocked with institutional soap, razor blades, toilet paper, hairnets, safety pins, floor wax, shaving cream and, last but not least, government cheese.

The smell of adobo and fish was always there.

Grandma's voice was sharp but gentle. "Anthony, come and eat your lunch, bring little Anthony." I followed my Uncle slowly.

"Don't be ashamed, brown boy. You'll pay off these free meals in due time."

"Be quiet and eat," Grandma would say.

The rice and chili and the sinigang were delicious and the sweat would pour from our foreheads. I especially loved the little bowls filled with soy sauce and green chili peppers. It made us sweat even more.

I'd mostly sit and listen to my Uncle talk. "Hey, boy, you know you as green as a pool table and twice as square." And he'd sweat more and Grandma would bring me more adobo.

"Let me tell you, young blood, we were from Fillmore. It was like Spanish Harlem on the east coast. A whole neighborhood of black and brown folks, only difference was that in Spanish Harlem you had Puerto Ricans and in Fillmore it was 'Flips.' A lot of Filipino brothers married black sisters so we had some beautiful Filipino-black sisters and they had some niggah-flip babies like you, baby boy."

Now I began to laugh and sweat at the same time. "You had mom-

and-pop grocery stores owned by Chinese and Japanese in the neighborhood and you had jazz clubs all on 'the set,' you know. The cops were afraid to come down to the 'mo."

Grandma placed more adobo on Uncle Anthony's plate. "You're talking crazy, kid," Grandma volunteered.

"I'm trying to tell this brown baby boy something, Ma. Look, blood, most of the dudes I ran with was brothers. We had our clubs and we had gang warfare but it ain't like it is now. We fought from the shoulders, one on one."

I continued to sweat in the steam from the hot rice.

"I used to see Malcolm in Fillmore. It was like the Harlem of the west coast. They had Flip gangs that ran around Fillmore in the '40's. They were players. They were from the families of the first Flips that got here, like your Grandma with her African nose."

Grandma just shook her head. " They wore zoot suits and had their hair slicked back and laid to the side."

My uncle preferred to wear an Afro and continued to wear one long after it went out of style. I just listened and thought, "How would I ever be able to live up to all of this?"

At that point we'd both finished our food. Uncle Anthony hugged me and gave me a kiss, "I love you, baby boy." And Grandma said we were both crazy. I think about those times a lot, and so does Uncle Anthony.

Tony Robles

---

sinigang, sour soup with fish or pork, and vegetables

adobo, marinated meat with condiments

zoot suit, pre-WWII fashionable men's wear

THE PIG

Brenda Manuel

The killing and roasting of a pig was common in our backyard. Many of my father's Filipino male friends would arrive early at the house. They would gather in the backyard to choose the fattest pig, set up the fire and pit in the ground and boil huge pots of water to scale and scrape off the pig's hair before roasting. This was a common event that took place during celebrations such as weddings, births, baptisms, communions and holidays.

As a little girl, I would watch from the window and was never allowed to go outside with "the men." But I liked listening to them laugh and talk while they prepared for the roasting of the pig.

My story is the one time my father allowed me to go with him.

Once when I was little, maybe five or six, I put on my small boots and ran after my father outside in the wet fog. He wore his boots. I followed behind, looking at the black rubber of his boots covered with dried mud. I quickly caught up with him and got hold of his hand as he went into the barn.

He told me that I was a big girl now and I could see him kill the pig today. It was still wet and foggy outside but the sun's rays were filtering through the clouds and the sky was brighter.

My father led the pig out to an open area and I followed behind. We went to the side of the barn. I watched as my father tied the pig's legs closely together. The pig lay on its side and I watched as my father cut the pig's neck with a long blade and he filled a large, flat pan with the pig's blood.

I closed my eyes when my father took the knife and began to cut open the pig's stomach. My father's rubber boots were now splattered with blood and so were mine. When I opened my eyes, I looked up and saw my father shaking his head back and forth and looking very sad. Then he pulled out from the inside of the pig's stomach, a clear sack of baby piglets stuck together. He showed me the babies.

He dragged the pig by its legs to the back of the barn while I stared at the baby pigs. There were six babies in that sack. My father came for the babies and took them to the back of the barn with the mother pig. He then washed down my boots with the water hose and told me to go back into the house.

UNCLE TOTO

Loralei Cruz Osborn

"I have reflected better and I believe that fulfilling the thoughts of my father is worth more than weeping for him, more than avenging him... "
- Jose Rizal, *Noli Me Tangere*

If a life has ended does its story also end? The life of Marianito Angeles Cruz ended before I can remember ever calling him "Uncle Toto." Yet, I carry within me his story and hope to one day tell others about his life, in essence, his story. The story of my uncle is not only about struggle for freedom, but also about the fusion of thoughts between two people, of my uncle's with mine as I put the pieces of his life together and continue to understand what it means to be Filipino American.

The story:

In the complete darkness of night, I am running. I am fleeing and trying to escape the evils chasing after me. From the sounds of the footsteps I imagine the fierce, large bodies attached to them. Breathing becomes more difficult as the exertion intensifies and applies its force on my lungs. My eyes are wide and searching wildly for refuge, though I know none really exists, at least not for long.

I go to the bridge where my father's name, Iluminado Cruz, is placed upon it and there I seek shelter. I breath in deeply and I think about my father and how this bridge was dedicated to him. How ironic it was for him to have died while trying to save the lives of others when a bomb from a Japanese fighter plane struck the hospital where he worked. Many people who live in Navotas have said the bridge should really be named after Nanay Flora, through whose heroic determination raised four children while continually searching for, but never finding, the remains of her husband.

Nestled between the concrete above and the large wooden piles below I feel safe as I watch the lights reflecting on the river. The lights are dancing and flickering like the fireflies my brother and I often chased when we were children. Slowly the lights are extinguished as if the fireflies are being caught one by one.

Recalling the words my mother repeated often since I was a child, "knowing where you came from will help you remember what you need to do and where you need to go," I think about my home and life in

Navotas. I also think about my family in the Philippines and in the United States. Finally, enveloped by a nostalgic sense of peace, I surrender to the black of night and fall asleep.

The memories return. When I awaken, I try to see through the darkness and cannot remember where I am. I soon realize that I am not in Navotas. As the objects around me come into focus, so do the memories.

It is 1973, I am four years old and too young to understand who Nixon is, where Vietnam is or how far away is the Philippines. I do not understand the disruption which occurs in our quiet home in the suburbs of Maryland. Everything happens so quickly. My mother answers the phone; shaken, she gives the phone to my father. I hear him cry for the first time. My older brother, sister and I are told that dad's youngest brother, Uncle Toto, has died.

My mother explains "We need to pray for Uncle Toto." I am frightened when I hear the trembling in my father's voice as he recites the Lord's Prayer. After he is done, I wait for a moment and ask timidly "How did he die, Daddy?" That question has been posed once again.

Twenty years later, when my father has a heart attack, a wave of urgency sweeps over me. I have so many questions about where and how he grew up, about his family, questions he answered through the many stories he told me when I was too young to appreciate or remember them. I feel I do not know enough about him and his Filipino culture. I realize how precious my heritage is to me by foreseeing it forever lost to the past.

Attending to my father while he is recuperating at home, we have many conversations about Uncle Toto. We look through old photo albums and pictures. There are a few old photographs of Uncle Toto visiting our home in Maryland and I notice his serious demeanor and the far away look in his eyes. My father and I also find a few of Uncle Toto's research papers. The more somber discussions between my father and I are about Uncle Toto's demise in the Philippines.

Marianito Angeles Cruz. Uncle Toto was born on December 8, 1939. In January of 1973, four months after martial law was declared, he died at the age of 34. Uncle Toto was highly regarded in our family and I remember words such as "intellectual" or "philosophical" and "brilliant" were used closely before or after his name was mentioned. After receiving his bachelors and masters degrees from the University of the Philippines (UP), Uncle Toto went to Providence, Rhode Island. He had been chosen for a fellowship program in mathematics at Brown University. While Uncle Toto studied in the United States, he and his professor, Jack Hale, wrote several papers, including one entitled "Asymptotic Behavior of Neutral Functional Differential Equations" in 1969, one of the papers my father and I tried and failed to decipher.

Shortly after completing his studies, Uncle Toto returned to the Philippines to teach mathematics at UP. The early 1970's in the Philippines marked a time of fear and rage for those persons who spoke publicly against the imposition of martial law. My uncle was not exempt. Although the details of my uncle's death are not clear and there is a chance I may never uncover the truth, his short but impassioned life must not be forgotten. To me, my uncle's life symbolizes discovery and truth and I believe in fulfilling his thoughts.

The Filipino American Experience. Recording the events of my uncle's life enables me to not only capture the accomplishments of a man who had much to offer, but also gives me a chance to further understand and retain my Filipino heritage. The experiences I have described are perhaps not too different from many Filipino Americans who are affected by the lives and stories of family thousands of miles away or generations apart. However, the Filipino American experience is comprised of an intricate and beautiful tapestry of stories and my story, interwoven with my uncle's is only one small piece within.

---

nanay, mother

AND THEN THERE WAS ONE

Mel Orpilla

Growing up in Bauang, La Union, the seven sons of Leon and Liberata Orpilla lived the lives of poor farmers. They helped their family by working their plot of land next to the ocean. I visited Bauang in 1986 and it was much the same as it has been for many generations. The road fronting their barangay led to the houses the Orpilla family called home. Behind the houses were vegetable, tobacco and other crops. And beyond that was the ocean where they fished. Visiting Bauang and seeing my roots brought me closer to my present...

My father Nazario and his two brothers, Modesto and Clemente, came to America in the mid-1920's. Like many of the Pinoys coming to America, they were looking for a better life. Their life here would be one of hard work, years as unmarried men, and finally the happiness of raising a family. My father and uncles symbolized the life of the manong. Today, only my father is left of the three who settled in Vallejo.

By 1939, the three brothers had secured jobs at Mare Island Naval Shipyard. To my father and uncles and to the many Pinoys who worked there before and after that time, a job at Mare Island became the path to a better life. So instead of working as farm laborers or as domestic servants, as they had in the past, the brothers had a secure job with the potential to become American citizens. They and other Filipinos working at Mare Island laid the foundation for the Filipino community in Vallejo as we know it today.

Many of the Pinoys lived in boarding houses in old Vallejo during the pre-World War II years. The other men living in the boarding houses became their compadres for life. Growing up, I called them either "uncle" or ninong. The many sepia colored photographs that I have collected show the men in their finest zootsuits or crowded in a small living room celebrating a birthday or other festivity.

In their spare time, the brothers fished. To earn extra money, they picked fruit on the weekends or my father worked part-time in a cafeteria on Mare Island.

Clemente was the first to get married, in 1935. He was the first Filipino allowed to get married at St. Vincent's Catholic Church. Modesto followed soon after. My father remained single until 1959. Because my father served in the U.S. Navy during World War II as a steward, he was allowed to bring a wife to America as a non-quota immigrant according to the War Brides Act passed in 1946. He met, fell in love with, and proposed to my mother through letters. My father was 53 years old and my mother, Ofelia, was 22.

In the 1970's, the Filipino population in Vallejo started to grow dramatically. In the old days, all the Filipino families knew each other. Now, all of a sudden, new faces and new "attitudes" have come into Vallejo. The vast majority of those moving to Vallejo were the professional Filipinos who immigrated after the restrictions were relaxed in 1965.

The past ten or so years have been very hard for my father. It seemed like he was attending funerals every weekend. The men who lived with him at the boarding house are all but gone. Uncle Johnny, Ninong Pete, and all the others, they're gone now. Only my father and Uncle George are left. Then in 1994 my dad's brother Clemente died at age 92. This year in 1995, my uncle Modesto passed away… His death cast a shadow on my father's mortality. I used to think they would all live forever. I never saw them get old.

My father turned ninety on his birthday, July 27, 1996. His legacy and that of the manong need to be remembered and revered. It amazes me that in a few years there will be no manongs left. My father and uncle lived extraordinary lives. Yet to them it was just living. Now…their life stories are no longer unknown and unsung. Time is running out for the manongs and for my father. Soon there will be only one manong left.

---

from Beyond Lumpia and That Bamboo Dance, The Filipino Experience, *Hayward Unified School District, April 1998 barangay,* (also baranggay, balangay), literally means boat, refers to community

Pinoy, adaptation of 'Filipino' ['pino(y)] popularized in the U.S. during the 1920's by immigrants in reference to their fellow countrymen

manong, older brother, Filipino adaptation of Spanish 'hermano', further adapted by Filipino Americans adding 's' (manongs) to refer to elderly Filipinos who pioneered immigration to the U.S.

compadre, godfather or male sponsor in a baptism or wedding

ninong, a godchild's reference to his/her godfather

zootsuit, fashionable men's wear in pre-WWII era

I AM

Herb Jamero

I AM a man of color descended from generations baked by a relentless Pacific sun. Tempered by balmy breezes and steamed by lush tropical forests. A color to be worn with pride and dignity. A color with different descriptions and wide ranging implications.

I AM a Malayan man of the islands - before a far away foreign king gave my people his name. Exploring and claiming these islands for my own. A proud warrior of the clan gathering together in isolated islands, mountains, and valleys never to know my brothers on the other side or across strange waters.

I AM a man whose forebears labored and tilled in ankle deep waters following a faithful plodding beast; climbed the arching coconut tree for its juices and fiber; cleared a landscape to build a shelter; and fished the surrounding seas.

I AM a man of the islands whose ancestors greeted waves of invaders who were to forever leave their mark on my people. First from the fabled city-states of Cathay, Mecca and Bombay, who came to trade, then stayed. Only to be overwhelmed by a race wearing metal and carrying both cross and sword. Cossack robed men of Castile vowing to Christianize and civilize. Then into Manila Bay steamed the Amerikanos on their own mission to rid us of the yoke of Spanish colonialism only to be replaced by Yankee imperialism. More recently, combating a race of samurai in an attempt to include us in their scheme for a greater "Asian Co-Prosperity Sphere."

I AM a traveled Manilaman forced to sail the great galleons carrying spices and gold across a great ocean to the New World. Whose sons were indentured to the sprawling plantations of other islands, then recruited to work the fields and canneries along the Pacific's eastern shore.

I AM a Pinoy of humble beginnings. Born to a generation of pioneers whose only dream was to make a better life for themselves and for those who carried their family name. Whose only possessions were carried in their memory, their hearts and their soul. Sacrificing an older and more traditional way for the new challenges in a more temperate land.

I AM a Filipino man, made rich by inherited traditions from generations past. Where strong family kinship, bonds of community, respect for elders and hospitality bind us forever fast.

I AM a Pilipino man, a blending of diverse peoples and equally diverse ways. Through my veins run the Christian values of Europe, the democratic values of America, and the spiritual values of Asia and the subcontinent of India. This colorful tapestry then to be sown and gathered by that lingering Malayan breed into a unique people.

I AM a hyphenated man, a Filipino-American who never learned the lyrics of his parents' language but remained in touch with his roots and his heritage. Torn but united by diversity. Stirred by nimble fingers and strumming simple love songs then awakening to an orchestra of different notes and sounds. Inspired by the oral histories of a far away land and its people while memorizing the history of a new world. A living collage of the past, present and future.

I AM an American man of Philippine origin not unlike the mestizo of the islands who became the leaders and models that placed this archipelago into the arena of modern nations. Our destiny and future to be forever entwined with that new race of mestizo – the ultimate mix of East and West....

I AM A MAN.

SECTION II
Urban Pinoy

THE MIGHTY MANHATTAN-BORN PINAY

Jeanette Gandionco Lazam

The year was 1949. We were already three years into the baby boomer craze, the United States was in its 1950's "prosperity" period, and at St. Clare's Hospital in midtown Manhattan, another boomer was born. This baby, named after the 1930's singer, Jeanette MacDonald, and her godmother, Gladys, was one of the few Filipinas born in Manhattan during that period. This is the story of her life....well, actually my life.

What makes my birth so historically significant and why am I writing about it? Actually nothing at all, except for the fact that very little has been written about the history of Filipinos in New York during the 1950's. What better way to introduce this topic than from someone who was born and raised in Manhattan's Lower East Side soon after the war ended, and the Korean War loomed over the horizon.

The Filipino community of New York City has often had its photos in Asian American history books - mainly of the young and handsome Filipino men – or referenced when talking about Queens, New York. But very little has been written about us, especially those living and working in the heart of NYC, namely the borough of Manhattan where it all started for the Filipino population.

I used to think that my father, who came to New York City in 1927 because he wanted to get off the farm, wanted to experience fast living, see what America was all about, work, send money home and probably have a romp in bed with a 'white-American woman.' I am sure my father came here for most of those reasons and more.....that is, aside from winning a scholarship to Fordham University. But my father was an urban man from Manila, filled with notions and dreams that most young men had at the turn of the century. And what better place to fulfill his dreams than abroad, in the place he had read so much about, the United States.

I had numerous opportunities to talk with my father before he died in 1971. I'm glad he told me his story and the stories of his compadres as well. It is a very different story than the stories of the manongs who came and settled on the west coast. Why? Because my father's story is very urban, complete with the fancy hotels, high-class bars, supper clubs, high-stake rollers, loose ladies of the night, and not-so-loose white ladies who found love and comfort with their Filipino lovers.

In the Roaring Twenties, New York was the place to be, and be seen in. Imagine the letters written to mothers and fathers back in the Philippines, of the life and times in New York. Imagine these young Filipino men, dressed in their finest double-breasted suits, starched white shirts, two-tone shoes, wide brimmed hats and long woolen overcoats. But, however well dressed these men were and spoke fluent English, according to Dad, the 'good life' they had read so much about was only for the rich and mainly white population. As such, Dad could never recollect any Filipino who became rich and prosperous during the 1920's.

Instead, back then, the living and working conditions of Filipino men on the East Coast mirrored that of their fellow compadres on the West Coast: segregated housing, ten to fifteen to a room, sharing everything including taking turns sleeping on one to two beds. Most of the men lived in Manhattan in and around mid-town (E. 50's to lower E. 60th streets), where many of the single-resident occupant (SRO) hotels were located. In order to accomplish this feat, some worked during the day, while others worked at night. This way the beds were shared, the living space was not as congested, and by pooling their resources together they had enough money to buy food and other items they needed.

✳   ✳   ✳

My father married my mother in the Philippines during the close of WWII, and had one child, my older sister, Maria. While he journeyed back to the United States from the Philippines to receive his dispatch orders, my mother began her preparations to follow the same trans-Pacific route, land in Seattle, Washington, and take the train cross country to meet my father in New York City. Once there, he escorted her to his new dwelling, a hotel near Columbus Circle, and there they would stay until public housing opened up in 1954. My family now had a new home, the Jacob Riis Housing Projects at 108 Avenue D, apartment 7A, on the Lower East Side of Manhattan.

We were one of two Filipino families that settled in the newly-built housing projects dotting the Lower East Side. There were at least forty to fifty buildings that made up Jacob Riis and Lillian Wald Housing Projects; an additional 50 to 60 buildings were part of the Peter Stuyvesant, Peter Cooper and Grand Avenue Cooperatives which ran along E. 14th Street and Avenue A/B/C, and Grand Avenue and Houston streets. Over 200 buildings and only two Filipino families! Not much by way of a Filipino community!

This was the era of Levittowns, those affordable box-shaped, pre-fab homes that dotted the suburban landscapes across the United States aptly named after the guy who invented the model city, Mr. Levitt. Selling at a low of $7,000, many returning G.I.'s took advantage of their G.I. loans and purchased the affordable housing. The Levittown housing communities were built in clusters simulating the affect of small towns. This housing came with front and back yard, picket fence, nearby school, churches, shopping centers......you name it, they had it. It was a complete neighborhood and one could buy into that neighborhood for practically nothing!

My father, was certainly due his G.I. benefits, but Dad was one of those peculiar fellows: wanted a family, but didn't want the economic responsibility of owning a house. Thus, his fear of owning a home and even a car, left the Lazam family as one of the very few Filipino families that never owned a house or car. As a matter of fact, we lived in rental units until my father passed away and my mother moved back to the Philippines.

I never understood why my father never wanted to buy a house or car. Every other Filipino family that I knew in the greater New York area had a house and car....we didn't. It seemed as though my father's dream of a good life did not include a mortgage or car loan. My mother longed to have a little nest she could call her own somewhere in Queens or perhaps Staten Island. She dreamed about having a car that would take her shopping and visiting friends. My mother was ready to buy into the American Dream of debt. Even when we finally made the move to the West Coast in 1965, there was no car to be bought and no house to be owned. We were a public transportation and rental unit family....and proud of it!

Public housing was safe when I was a kid. It had real honest-to-goodness playgrounds where parents sat on wooden benches and watched their children play. The Good Humor and Softee Ice Cream man came by everyday to sell their delicious ice cream. There was also the bagel, hot candied apple and Sabretts Hot Dog men....all friendly and known by the mothers sitting on the playground bench. It was a world that allowed young people to think, to aspire, to dream of the future...it was safe then.

Public school was the hip place to be. You didn't dare be found in a private parochial school that required uniforms and had the snobbiest students I ever encountered. My most exciting times were spent in public school, meeting new children, sharing experiences, having my first crush on a boy, then on a girl! It was a fun time where each classroom had day-outings or visits to the multitude of New York museums, the Botanical Garden in Brooklyn, Bronx Zoo, theatre and a host of other cultural expositions.

✳ ✳ ✳

Most New York City streets in the 1950's were cobblestone - hard on the feet and harder on a horse's hooves. In Manhattan, fresh produce, meat and fish were brought into the designated city market areas by horse-drawn cart. Every once in a while, you could either smell or see the horse shit on the streets, and it was surely a sad day to be the unfortunate one to step into a heaping pile of horse shit!

All along Avenue C, the outdoor market was filled with fruit and vegetable vendors, yelling out the days produce and price. Just inside the buildings were open stalls where the meat vendors and fish mongers all did the same thing: yell about their catch and price by pound. As noisy and loud as the open market could be, I never failed in joining my mother when she shopped there. I found just being in the midst of all this chaos, yelling, money exchanging and gossip so very exciting.

Further down Avenue C were the clothiers and bulk material vendors. The clothiers sold everything from lace handkerchiefs of the finest Irish linen, to real, honest-to-goodness dungarees in light blue and basic navy blue. The bulk material vendors sold any fabric you could think of. Inside their shops were bolts and bolts of lace, brocade, linen, cotton, embroidery, and every size and shape sewing needle. These vendors always had their sleeves rolled up, wore a gray or brown faded vest; on their heads they wore woolen caps or hats, and they always had a measuring tape dangling from their neck.

With their thick European mingled with a New York accent, these vendors could sell the shirt off your back and you wouldn't even know it. They had a sale angle for every customer, a pitch for every woman, a persistence that followed you around the store and out into the streets with promises of "You're never going to get a better deal than this." But most of all, they had character. That's really what made New York's Lower East Side so colorful and lively...the people who lived and worked there were all characters with distinct personalities.

The Lower East Side of Manhattan was predominantly European and Jewish. That mixture was reflected in what I call the "flavor" of the times. You were hard pressed not to find a small grocery store that didn't sell wooden barrel dill pickles, a deli that sold real kosher products, a candy store that sold egg cremes, lime rickies and two-cent seltzer, and best of all, a bagel man who sold hot bagels for only five cents. All of these establishments were either owned or operated by Jewish proprietors.

Orthodox Jews were everywhere. Men wore paes (sideburns) and long scraggly beards, dark-rimmed hats and long coats. The women and girls wore long-sleeved dresses, a kerchief wrapped around their head to cover their hair, full length black nylons and shoes reminescent of the styles worn during the 1800's. They were very religious, observing all the high holy days and always in prayer. Strictly kosher, pork never touched their lips and milk products were separated and served on special plates.

Then there were the Reformed Jews who sometimes ate Chinese egg rolls which meant that pork touched their lips, mouth, throat and landed in their tummys. I always asked my friend Lois how come she and her family ate pork and other Jews didn't. She always had a very simple explanation for that, "Because my family and I like Chinese food." End of question.

But whether Orthodox or Reformed Jews they gathered every Friday night at the temple. On Saturdays, Jewish parents sent their children to Shule or Hebrew School. For the boys it was especially important because they were preparing for their bar mitzvah, the Jewish celebration of when a boy becomes a man.

All along the Lower East Side, or for that matter in the greater New York area, there were enough synagogues (Jewish Temples) to match the mushrooming store fronts of Penticostal Churches that were springing up all over the place.

Because I very seldom ran into other Filipinos or had friends that were Filipino, growing up in the housing projects was for me a life of a Filipino cum Jewish. Though my mirror told me I was Filipino, my experiences told me I was Jewish.

✳   ✳   ✳

Once a month my mother would give us a shot in the arm of what Filipino culture was like. We would take the uptown train, find ourselves in mid-town Manhattan, and make our way to the Filipino Community Center of New York. There, my mother would meet up with her friends. We would eat all the Filipino food our tummy's could hold and then sit on the sidelines and listen to the old-timers play their music. That was the extent of Filipino culture for me. Other times we would visit my parent's friends, Joe and Valine and their son Ritchie, who owned a small coffee shop on the East 70's, my sister and I would eat food while my parents caught up on all the gossip. I could never remember how we got back to our apartment or how I managed to be tucked into bed. What I did remember was my mother saying, "Jeanette, why don't you go take a nap upstairs while Valine and I talk?" Next thing I knew, we were home! All told, I think my mother had about three to four good friends she kept in constant communication with and visited when time permitted. All of her friends were from Leyte, the island where she was born. They came over to the United States soon after the war and settled, mainly in Manhattan, Queens and Governor's Island, a military base.

Learning the 'language' was not something my parents were into teaching us, nor were there classes at any of the schools or after school facilities that were teaching language, specially not Tagalog. So, my sister and I were left to our own imagination to figure out what my parents were saying when they reverted to the 'vernacular.' It was obvious to us that whatever they talked about had to be important or only for the ears of adults. But, like any language, if you keep on hearing the same words with the same emotion attached to it, it was a good bet that sooner or later you'd be able to figure out what folks were saying, even if what you understood was very limited. For instance, "kumusta ka?" I'd hear that phrase each time my mother got on the phone or see one of her Filipino friends. That also applied to my dad when he met up with his buddies or talked with them on the phone.

Then there were the violent, angry phrases like, "punyita," "punyitero," "pisting yawa," and of course the good ol' mixed Visayan-English phrase of, "Yawa, you wait until your father comes home!" All of the violent and angry phrases were accompanied by pure and unadulterated physical gyrations like waving the arms in mid air, facial stares of agony, and grabbing your arm, lifting you off the floor or sofa (whichever was available at the moment), and taking whatever inanimate object was at arms reach and wacking it across your butt. All the while you were screaming as if someone was murdering you!

I remember one time my mother was so angry at me for breaking her vase that she completely lost it. *"Punyitero! Tigas ng ulo!"* She grabbed my arm and started wacking me with the stems of her artificial roses. Geez, was I tore up after that one. In about two hours, she began to feel guilty and dragged me into the bathroom (I was still crying in the corner of my room) and applied, of all things, rubbing alcohol! I thought I would die! She said she needed to do that just in case infection set in!

During that particular beating episode, she must have shouted every single known and unknown Tagalog and Visayan curse word she could think of. Man, she was wacking away at me, all the way down the hallway, into my room, and finally wedged me between my bed and the closet. Oooooh, I tell you I was in pain. But, I got to know a few more words in Visayan, which later on in life proved useful while I was living in Cebu and having a discussion with a cab driver about why I thought he was cheating me.

✳ ✳ ✳

It was as common to have one's hair done up at a beauty parlor on a Saturday, as it was to eat an ice cream cone on a hot summer New York day. On one such Saturday, my mother made an appointment to have her hair washed, dried, cut and curled at 9:00 am. My sister was at a friend's apartment, my father was getting ready for work, and I was too young to be left by myself, so there was no choice but to drag me along and wait while my mother beautified herself.

The beauty parlor was already packed when we arrived, and the hum of the dryers filled the shop that you could barely hear over the din of noise. My mother took me by the arm and warned me profusely not to get in the way of the attendants. If I wanted to play I had to play outside right in front of the shop so she could keep her eye on me. I started toward the door and proceeded to vanish from her radar screen. One hour into the beautification of my mother, I was already dreaming of an ice cream cone. So, I went back inside, asked my mother for a quarter, she picked up her handbag, searched around until she found one and warned me not to mess up my tee shirt and shorts. I nodded with an affirmative yes.

The candy store was a few feet away from the beauty parlor which meant that I didn't have to cross any streets. At that time all things on God's good earth were inexpensive, including ice cream cones. A double scoop of two different flavors on a sugar cone cost 25 cents. I asked the man behind the counter if I could have one scoop of chocolate and the other strawberry.

He took his ice cream scooper and dug deep into the container filled to the brim with ice cream. The scoops were larger than life which meant that I had to do twice the amount of licking in a speed faster than a speeding bullet. I knew I could keep that ice cream from dripping down the side of the cone as I had done so many times before. But I had not banked on the temperature of the day and the heat inside the beauty parlor.

The man gave me my cone and I immediately started to lick it like mad. But no matter how fast and furious I licked the damn thing, the melt down was faster than my tongue could keep up with. By the time I returned to the beauty shop, ice cream was pouring all around the cylinder of the cone. I turned toward my mother in fright, fearing that it would drip onto the floor of the shop. For the next few moments everyone and everything around me appeared as if they were in slow motion. Mother dug deep into her handbag frantically looking for a tissue. She got up from her seat and raced toward me, tissue in hand. I took one big lick of that cone and the ice cream came tumbling down. SPLAT!

I tried to catch the remains of the ice cream in my hand. I even got on my knees to prevent the ice cream from hitting the floor. With everyone watching, Mother rushed toward me with her tissue and a hush came upon the shop that was almost deadening.

There we were. Mother in her curlers, me on the floor and the ice cream cone melting into a sea of chocolate and strawberry. A yell came from the corner of the shop. "Lady, is that your daughter?!" cried the proprietor of the shop. My mother, looking toward her answered, "Yes." Not wasting another breath, the beauty shop owner said in the meanest tone, "You get on your knees and clean that mess up!" Mother shrunk in embarrassment.

Mother quietly went to the back of the shop, got a wet rag, came back and wiped up the mess. All the while the other patrons and some of the attendants murmured, "These foreigners, who do they think they are?

They come into our shop, mess things up. Who did they think was gonna clean that slop off the floor...us?"

I knew my mother heard every single word. She was humiliated, but there was nothing she felt she could do. Quietly, she cleaned up my mess, washed out the rag and returned to her chair under the hair dryer.

✳   ✳   ✳

Still not having a clue as to what and who Filipinos were, my ethnic identity changed again from being a Filipino-Jew, to a Filipino-Puerto Rican. The foundation (upon which I laid my weary head) that supported my Filipino identity was still very shaky. Thus, whatever the dominant culture of the Lower East Side was, I became. I admit, this made life for me very difficult, always having to change my ethnic identity every few years. But I had to because I just didn't have any other role model. So, for the next five to ten years, I became a Filipino-Puerto Rican...which, by all accounts was closer in racial and historical similarity than being a Filipino-Jew.

Ever had a cuchifrito? Do you even know what one looks like? Neither did I until those greasy, deep-fried critters started showing up in the small two-by-four restaurants directly across the street from my projects. They smelled like old used frying oil, and looked even nastier....kinda like fried octopus with its tentacles hanging all over the place. But once you tasted one, you never forgot. Not that the taste was wonderful or great....you simply never forgot that rancid oil taste. However, it was the big hit of the day in the mid-1950's, and with a bottle of ice cold Coca-Cola during the hot summer months, ya' just couldn't beat that combination.

I still preferred to eat hot dogs myself, and with cold slaw as the topping, shoved that puppy down with an icy bottle of Pepsi (never did care for Coke). But sooner or later I knew that I would have to taste a cuchifrito. It's a funny thing about getting to know a new cultural and racial group of people. First there are the stares (at one another), then the smiles, and if there's an attraction, you might even get a courtship dance going. After all that comes the talk, the walk and the food. Food has got to be the one item that eventually breaks through all the garbage and tough talking shit.

Like the time I got to know Irma de Leon. She was probably one of the cutest girls in my building and probably the entire block. She was always having boyfriends and friends surrounding her. In the afternoons, right after school, I would run upstairs to my apartment, change clothes and meet her and other friends downstairs. Generally we'd just hang out and talk, but sometimes, she would invite all of us up to her apartment on the fourth floor and whaddya know, her mother would be cooking. Geez, you could smell Mrs. De Leon's cooking a mile a way. It was awesome!

We'd get inside her house and I would hope and pray that her mother would offer whatever she was cooking. Well, Puerto Rican and Filipino families are similar; they can't invite someone to their place and not feed them. Bingo...food on the table! And with that, our tummys were full, our laughter was hardier, and whatever tension we may have been feeling at the time all got swallowed down in four bites of food and four big gulps. Food just has a way of pushing everything aside and making relations plain and simple. Know what I mean?

Anyways, for the next several years I took on the personal responsibility of searching out new and different Puerto Rican food, and making sure that I was hanging around Irma when her mother was busy cooking.

✳   ✳   ✳

No sooner did I find the square peg that fit into the round hole when my parents decided to move. I was absolutely devastated. How could I ever leave New York? Was there a world outside New York City? There couldn't be! But I was too young to be part of the decision-making process. It was up to my mother and father to figure out where the Lazam family was going to move. At one point, I heard talk of moving back to the Philippines. I panicked! I thought to myself, "How is this rough and tumble native New Yorker gonna ever make it in the Philippines?" I prayed to God that my parents wouldn't choose the Philippines. And man, did I ever pray.

After about a month or so of idle talk and opinion making, my father called us to the dining room table and announced that this family was moving to the west coast....San Francisco to be exact. The plan called for my mother, sister, brother and me to go ahead. We would find a suitable apartment, enroll in school and about a year later, my father would follow. On the one hand, I found the entire discussion of moving fascinating. On the other, my heart was breaking. How could my parents expect me to leave the city of my birth? New York was my home town, filled with all my friends and familiar sites, the best food in the world and the best city in the world! How could they do this to me?

All my life I spent walking the streets of Manhattan, sometimes even venturing into Brooklyn, the Bronx and Queens. I was just beginning to discover a world outside of the Lower East Side, and now, my parents wanted to move to San Francisco?! What in the hell is San Francisco, I thought? It couldn't possibly be like New York, a city that never shuts down and was exciting just about anywhere you went.

All I ever heard about San Francisco were those damn cable cars, beaches and Rice A-Roni! Little did I know that people never go swimming at San Francisco beaches, and the cable cars, well, big deal so they go up and down hills! So what? Those cable cars could never compare to the New York Subway that took you anywhere and everywhere you needed to go.

Just the thought of me moving to San Francisco felt as though the blood in my body was slowly draining out; I felt as though the spirit of my life was leaving me.....I had to do something real quick otherwise I would just roll up and die! At that very moment, I felt I should do everything I never did while growing up. You know how that is, just 'cause you live some place you kinda take for granted the sites that tourists go to visit. You figure, "Well, I'll be here all my life, there's time to see these places." Wrong!

For the next few months, I managed to visit every single museum, art gallery, icon, artifact, attraction New York had to offer. I was gonna make sure that my memory banks were filled with the sites, places, people and events that made New York the wonderful city that it was. I made sure that I knew every street, alley, corner, store on the Lower East Side, and equally made sure that I had pictures of Union Square and its famous stores, Kleins and Lanes. I felt as though I was moving through life at a pace of unbelievable proportion, and no matter how hard I tried, I was just not going to ever see and do everything I needed to see and do before I left for "sunny" California. Ah, the time was drawing near.

I truly think in the back of my mind as I looked, watched, gazed and was amazed, that I had not really known New York, that I was searching desperately for my "Filipino community," even though I never really found it in the fifteen years I lived in New York.

They say no matter what the loss, one grieves because one is hurt. And I can't begin to tell how hurt I was to leave my birth city, Manhattan. For years after we had settled down in San Francisco, I mourned and pined away for my New York City. I (at the time) felt I could never adjust to living on the West Coast, much less San Francisco. But they say "time heals" and righteously so.

Now I live in Oakland, California, with a partner, two parakeets and one ferral cat who loves me but refuses to show it. Would I ever move back to New York? Well, I did and guess what? The city never claimed my soul like it did when I lived there. I will always love New York City and continue to dream about the days where I was the only mighty, Manhattan-born Filipina of the Lower East Side. I know I will always cherish those days; talk about it as if my childhood was just around the corner. I will share to no end the stories of me and my friends and our escapades and forays into the Upper East and West Sides, our first time shopping in Macy's, Union Square, egg cremes, lime rickeys and pretzels. I will share until the day I die what it was like growing up on the Lower East, being a Filipino and searching everyday of my life for the Filipino community.

I do believe one is a product of their environment. New York still lives on inside of me and each time I visit, I just pick up where I last left off. And the story of the Mighty, Manhattan-Born Filipina of the Lower East Side will keep on goin' until there's no more New York or Filipino left inside of me to tell.

Between you and me, I doubt that will ever happen!

OF PIPES, TOBACCO, DAD

Victoria J. Santos

An old, Danish smoking pipe sits on a white bookcase in my office. It is small and compact, with a short black stem and smooth brown bowl. I bought it for my father from a small tobacco and pipe shop in Copenhagen while on vacation one year. I can still see his easy smile as he cupped the bowl in his dark brown hand, its skin weathered by years of hard work. Dad took such pleasure in carefully packing his favorite cherry blend tobacco into that pipe, lighting up, and then slowly savoring that first draw of aromatic smoke. Once I gave him a bottle of Grand Marnier and watched in surprise as he laid some tobacco out on paper on the kitchen table and sprinkled it with some of the liqueur. He claimed that it made his smoke smooth and sweet.

Dad wasn't always a pipe smoker. He switched to smoking pipes later in life. It seemed to fit the leisure time he fell into after working non-stop for most of his life. During his working years, he enjoyed Corina Lark cigars. Dad knew tobacco. Born in 1901, he grew up on his family's tobacco farm in Laoag, Ilocos Norte. He said he started smoking as a kid, as if it was the most natural thing to do.

At fifteen, he struck out for Manila where he worked in a bakery for a few years. When my older brother Ron and I were younger, we watched Dad as he sifted flour together with baking powder, adding other ingredients to make wonderfully light waffles or some delectable dessert. It seemed so natural for him but he never told us until years later that he worked as a baker. It was the beginning of a very long and varied work career for Dad.

In his late teens, he was hired in Manila by a Hawaiian sugar cane company to work in their fields. To qualify for the job, he said, "I had to demonstrate I could carry a hundred-pound sack." He was five feet tall and slender then and he weighed just about the equivalent of the sack, but he was strong. As Dad said proudly with a steady eye years later, "I wanted to go to Hawaii." Demonstrating how he planted his feet firmly on the ground and squared his shoulders, he said, "I braced myself, picked up that sack and slung it over my shoulder. The bosses also liked that I spoke both Ilocano and Tagalog so I got hired."

Shortly after, he was aboard a ship heading for Hawaii. A few days out to sea, he became feverish and quite ill. He was put off ship into an infirmary in Hong Kong to be treated. "I knew I would make it when I saw Jesus," Dad said. Deeply religious, he had had a vision of the Sacred Heart while he was ill and took it as a good sign. Mom said he was probably delirious from the fever but Dad swore he wasn't. A month later he was on another ship bound for Hawaii.

Dad lasted a month in Hawaii before deciding that the sugarcane fields weren't for him. He and a cousin who had joined him there made enough money from playing cards with the other workers, skipped out on their contract with the company, and took off for the mainland. His youthful quest for adventure and discovery continued. They landed in Seattle where they had some townmates they could stay with for a while. Hearing of jobs in the salmon canning factories in Alaska they went up there to work for a season. After that Dad became part of a railroad gang laying ties through the western states before migrating to Chicago. He arrived there in the mid-1920's.

My father only mentioned these things to me in his later years. His memory was quite sketchy about how long he actually spent in Alaska and in the west. In fact, throughout all the years I was at home we believed his birth date was March 3, 1903. It wasn't until he applied for social security benefits and had to write back to the Philippines for documentation that he learned his actual birth date was March 2, 1901. Most people might be stunned to learn that they were suddenly two years older but Dad just took it in stride.

In 1929, my mother, then seven years old, and grandmother followed my grandfather to Chicago two years after his arrival there. My grandfather had migrated from Tagudin, Ilocos Sur, to the States also in the mid-

1920's. He and two younger brothers worked in the salt mines in Utah but my grandfather contracted pneumonia from the mines, so they moved on to Chicago where he eventually became employed as a Pullman porter.

In the 1930's my grandparents ran a restaurant with a pool hall in the back which became a hang-out for many of the single young Filipino men. Dad had a barber shop close to the restaurant on State Street not far from Holy Name Cathedral, just north of downtown. Mom and Dad met when he started frequenting the restaurant.

My mother's family was one of the first Filipino families in Chicago. Mom was a rarity in the 1930's: a young Filipina of marriageable age, and she had caught my father's eye. When he wasn't working, Dad was always well groomed, wore tailored clothes and slicked back his jet black hair with pomade. He was handsome, had a warm smile and wonderful sense of humor, and was a good dancer. They began courting secretly her last year of high school. Knowing my grandparents would object to the 20-year difference in their ages, my parents eventually eloped in 1939, taking their vows at a side altar at Holy Name Cathedral. They took off for Muncie, Indiana where they had some friends, and Dad began barbering at a friend's shop. As the family story goes, my grandfather went after them with a shotgun. He and my grandmother eventually reconciled themselves to my parents' marriage after my mother became pregnant with my older brother.

In those first years of their marriage, Mom said Dad did most of the cooking because she didn't know how to cook the dishes he liked. She was content to let him cook and throughout my childhood and beyond,

Dad made most of the Filipino foods we enjoyed. The kitchen was his.

The week before my wedding in Chicago, my husband's parents and aunt arrived from Portugal and stayed at my parents' home. I wanted to cook a special meal for them on my own and started preparing a chicken tarragon dish my husband liked. Dad watched for a while, saying nothing, and then hauled out a huge pot and started boiling some crabs. He put on a large pot of rice and made a vegetable dish. As Dad saw it, that chicken wasn't going to be enough. I was a bit put out by this because I wanted to do this meal alone but as it turned out, Dad was right. The chicken would not have been enough. Furthermore, my father-in-law and his sister absolutely relished the crabs and to this day, he still remembers that meal.

Dad was indeed a jack-of-all-trades. He had a natural curiosity and learned by watching and doing. He worked at various times as a barber, carpenter, and photo retoucher - all trades he learned after arriving in the United States. In the 1950's, we lived in a predominantly black neighborhood on the near north side of Chicago. My father was making his living as a photographer by then - another trade he learned on his own - and he and my mother ran the studio together. Dad was the photographer for a number of church gospel choirs in the area. Occasionally, my brother or I went with Dad to help him with his equipment when he photographed the choirs or black weddings. The music was so lively compared to the staid hymns at our Catholic masses.

When Dad wasn't busy in the studio or out on appointments, he could sometimes be found at the local pool hall down the block, shooting pool with the regulars, chomping on his cigar. He was so easy-going, good-natured, and accepting of others, people instantly liked him. His size and accent never seemed to get in the way. He had an ingratiating way of addressing his larger black male neighbors or customers as "Chief" as in "How are you today, Chief?" or "Can I help you, Chief?" It always elicited a smile.

The last job Dad had before retiring was that of medical photographer, working first for the University of Illinois Dental School, then the University of Chicago Medical School. A friend who worked at the dental school had referred him to the first job and the second job followed several years later. He placed a high value on education for my brother and me. Indeed, he revered the dentists and doctors he worked with because they were so highly educated. By the end of his career, he actually had photo credits in medical journals and books. With only a fifth grade education he had exceeded his own expectations.

Becoming American citizens was also a milestone in both my parents' lives. Participating in the voting process was a real privilege for them. While Dad worked at various jobs, my mother eventually became active as a precinct worker for the Democratic Party. At the same time, they never ventured far from their Filipino roots.

Dad retired when he was in his sixties and lived to be 86 years old. In those years following retirement, he and my mother remained very active in a number of Filipino clubs in Chicago and generously devoted their time, money, and efforts in helping to buy a building for the Filipino Community Center on the north side of the city. Mom and her friends organized and ran weekly bingo games for 23 years at the center to raise money and Dad would cook up the food the players bought during the games. They raised $12,000 to $15,000 a year for the center, a sizeable contribution over the years. In the sixties they also helped to found the first Filipino credit union in Chicago. Dad was definitely a man who enjoyed being in motion. The week before he died, he was up on a ladder painting the garage on his own.

My father could be exasperating in his stubbornness at times. But mostly, he nurtured his family with far more than his cooking. He showered us with unconditional love. My brother and his children and I always knew how much he loved us because he was always there for us, beaming proudly at our accomplishments big and small, attending recitals and games, taking the time to listen to us.

When I think of my parents, I marvel at the incredible adaptability, resourcefulness, and faith that helped them survive a brutal ocean crossing, overwhelming homesickness, and a transition to a strange and new culture. Surviving the Great Depression, and certainly racism and bias, gave further proof of their strength and determination.

Throughout his life, Dad succeeded despite great adversity. He was forever open to new challenges and indeed, seemed to embrace them. He always seemed to know what he needed to do in life to survive. He always seemed at home in his universe. He always seemed to know who he was. He might not have felt or articulated these things himself, but it is my impression of him. Sometimes one never fully understands and appreciates the impact of a parent's life until one is fully grown, is faced with finding one's own way in the world, and has a child of one's own to guide and teach life's lessons.

Occasionally, the sweet aroma of someone's pipe tobacco will find its way to me. With wisps of smoke swirling around me, images unexpectedly swirl through my mind - of Dad cooking up a feast in the kitchen, dancing the rhumba with Mom, watching his grandchildren at play, or hammering away to build a storage cabinet in the garage of my first home. He was small, compact, and sturdy like the pipe I gave him. And like his cherished tobacco that permeated the air with its mellow, sweet fragrance, Dad permeated the many lives of all who knew and loved him, his presence lingering long after he left us.

The author with Dad on her wedding day, December 18, 1982

114

HOME GROWN, OAKLAND

Eleanor M. Hipol Luis

Walk from home to Chinatown
Chinatown to home, pass the holes
where the smelt run with the
water flowing from Lake Merrit
Pass Auditorium Village School
a fence away from the Red Cross shelter
where food and beds are free
Pass the projects where children
live and play until the sun goes down,
I want to move there.

Roller derby maniacs root for the
Bay Bombers at the Exposition Building where
Pepper Gomez and Kenji Shibuya wrestle
against Pat Patterson, the Cadillac King
While across the street Captain Satellite
lands in Peralta Park, as the crowds
line up wearing their newly shined shoes for
the event at the Oakland Auditorium.

Hobos aren't just on trains, they walk
to the Mission where you don't have to
beg or steal for food, then they jump onto a
train and wave to you if you wave first
Can't believe they would steal you

but the policeman woke me to ask if I saw the
little girl that was kidnapped.

Walked to St. Anthony's Sunday,
spoke Latin as one voice read from the
black missal and angels sang with
voices so high my ears pierced themselves
Somber ladies in black clicked wooden clothespins,
rosaries dangled from old hands and
young hands and from the mouths of babies
to keep them within the confines of the mass.

Walked to the other church, on First Avenue
sang loud and jumped up and down, threw up
my arms and said "Yes!" anytime it felt right,
shook hands with the man who raised
his voice and softened it to say 'Amen.'
Ran home with Alethia
chasing butterflies.

Third grade at Franklin wasn't like
Auditorium Village, unfamiliar faces
lined up where painted circles and
squares organized recess
Sixth grade teacher said "Go to Westlake;
more Chinese like you." Don't go EAST,
go WEST young lady.

116

I'm not Chinese, I'm Filipino.
Ya' know, P-h-i-l-i-p-p-i-n-e Islands
brown from the sun, eat gabi and grated coconut
lechon pigs in the backyard after we slit its throat
snapped those chicken necks, chopped off their heads
watched them run around our backyard
Stroked head the finest Cock whose razor blade
slit the neck of the weaker one
Here is my Philippine Islands!

Filipinotown is in Chinatown, Oakland
Baldo's poolhall racked 'em up——a long time
What's your pleasure 8-ball, poker, music?
a wash basin bass, and a saxophone and
upright piano that play slightly out of tune
Or eat chop suey at Elite cafe where the
Pinay waitress with a nice lookin' half
Chinese daughter treats you special.

Newcomers to the school, a girl with
three brothers sitting there so still and
quiet, wondering how long before
they will be at home. "Talk to them...you
do know their language, TAG-alog...you are
Filipino...run along now...and take them with you."
Damn, I might as well be Chinese
How do you speak Filipino—

Ilocano, Visayan, Pangasinan
Never heard of TAG-alog.

Now let's get this straight
I am Chicana, yo soy Chicana
my skin is brown, my hair dark and wavy
Spanish isn't foreign like Chinese
Only my tortilla is a lumpia wrapper
and we cook our mungo beans with pork,
shrimp or tiny dried fish, never refried.
Okay to come to my house
cause you look like me.

Went to the Rumpus Room via
Quick-Way for a burger and fries
stopped at Broadway Bowl to play pinball
sip Coke-a-Cola, scored the bowlers
smoked cigarettes in a non-smoke free environment
checked out the brown bruthas—-just hangin',
doin' nuthin' but lookin' so fine,
swingin' vices to win their fights
and speakin' Filipino.

Go back to the Vet's building, girl
where you can be supervised
speak only when permitted
dance-the-night-away doing the *Cariñosa*
the *Pandango sa Ilaw* or cha-cha-cha to

Cherry Pink and Apple Blossom White
look refined and someday be the queen of
American Legion.

Transition, Oakland to Alameda
island so different from my Islands,
minority among blue levi's and white t-shirts,
count us on your fingers
Linda, Ellie, Rosalyn, Nancy, Lourdes,
Rachel, Corazon, Domingo, Ernie, Danny,
Tony, Bobby, and one more here and there
PLEASE STAND UP AND BE COUNTED!

They knew I came from Oakland
asked me why I looked so hard
It was Maybelline, not Wendy Ward
black matched my hair, half up and
half down, tresses down my back
with a streak of red from the lemon and
peroxide, the higher the hair the taller
you looked——-from behind
Asked me did I hide
razor blades in my
Aquanet beehive,
choke chain in my sweater
sleeves, and
did I fight on the weekends.

Learned at Laney who sold what and how to buy
college you know – higher learning
where we played spades and hearts
danced at the noon hour in front of the BSU
where the bruthas 'n sistas played indoors
forkin' their 'fros while we shared Old English
'cause pappa had a brand new bag.

Drove to the City last night; Seven Hills
used my fake ID, wanderers croonin',
wall to wall flips dancin', stompin',
rappin', jive'n – damn slow down
roll'n and slow dancin', never knew
who was with who 'cause they never told you
Found out with a fist in your face
or a face in your face, or a word
in your face then you were
face to face with an attitude.

Drove home past Chinatown,
familiar place with memories of a
simple life passed on
Remembering all this
and all that and thinkin',
thinkin' I'm home grown and
don't get lost anymore.

gabi, taro root

lechon, roast pork

Cariñosa, traditional dance among Christianized Filipinos

Pandanggo sa Ilaw, traditional dance among Christianized Filipinos

PIEDMONT AVENUE

Benjamin Mendoza

Over the hill from Broadway and 40th Street is Piedmont Avenue. When I was growing up, this area was where the genteel people of the lower Oakland hills lived and shopped. When I and my friends ventured into this area, we affected a rough and tough attitude that was in contrast to the silent "you don't belong here" stare of the boys our own age that we met while on the Avenue. It was not difficult for us to notice that these boys were dressed in more expensive clothes than what we wore. A hill and two city blocks were all that separated our neighborhoods. It was a chasm determined by economics.

At 41st and Piedmont was the "C" Key System train station, one of the electric trains that crossed on the lower deck of the San Francisco-Oakland Bay Bridge. The covered open-ended building was crowned with a clock tower. In the triangular building below the clock tower was a restaurant that was always crowded during the early commute hours. Right across the street was a Bank of America where Mom banked. It was where I banked when I started college.

My favorite shop on the Avenue was Pearson's Hardware. It was located at 40th and Piedmont. Today the shop would be called old fashioned and very unusual in that every nook and cranny of the store was filled with odds and ends. Tubs, garden equipment, tools, spools of wire, and all sorts of items hung from the ceiling. There were bins, barrels, boxes, and multi-drawer cupboards located throughout the store and filled with every conceivable item whether useful, useless or obsolete. Narrow aisles compressed by things for sale snaked throughout the store. Finding an item sometimes demanded that a small section of the store be dismantled and then restacked once the item was found. There were probably tens of thousands of items in the store and Mr. Pearson knew where everything was. I used to like to go into the store just to find an item that I didn't know about and ask Mr. Pearson what it was used for. Mr. Pearson always had an answer although whether he told me the truth or just said it to get me off his back, I shall never know. I heard it said that if someone makes it, Pearson's has it or can get it for you.

Other stores on the Avenue that I remember included a five and dime store, a haberdashery and a small café. The business that always seemed to be busy was Fenton's Creamery located a block and a half west of Piedmont Avenue on 41st Street. During the school year the Creamery was the hangout of students who wore "Mickey Mouse shoes" (two-tone brown and white shoes). This was the "badge of belonging" for those students from well-to-do families who attended Piedmont and Oakland Technical High Schools and for those from other areas aspiring to be part of that group. The uniform for this group also included slacks instead of levis and a white cardigan sweater. After school, most tables at the Creamery were taken by these kids, leaving few tables available for the occasional drop-in students wanting to buy their favorite ice cream dish. There was no confrontation between these students and other groups wanting to use the Creamery after school. It was a case of simple economics. The few times the other groups wanted to use the Creamery, they just went at a different time. When one started dating, a movie and a soda meant a movie and a stop at Fenton's.

There were two other places that I went to on the Avenue. One was Saint Leo's Church and the other was the Piedmont Theater. The family attended Saint Leo's Church whenever we missed the mass at Sacred Heart Church. Whether by design or chance the masses at the two churches would begin a half-hour apart. Thus, if one missed the 7:30 mass at Sacred Heart, one could easily make the 8:00 mass at Saint Leo's. The walk to Saint Leo's took about fifteen minutes more than the walk to Sacred Heart. The Piedmont Theater on Piedmont Avenue and the Senator Theater on Telegraph Avenue had a convenient scheduling arrangement for the neighborhood as the churches we went to. If one missed a movie at the Senator, all you had to do was wait a week and the same double bill would be shown at the Piedmont. If you missed the movie at the Piedmont, you had one last chance to see the film and that was at the Chimes Theater on College Avenue.

My friends and I used to argue about where the best hamburgers were made. My choice was a hamburger place on the northeast corner of Piedmont and MacArthur Boulevard. The hamburgers there were big, juicy and filled with pickles, onions, and lettuce. This was also the place where I would buy hamburgers and french fries for my newspaper customer-patients in Kaiser Permanente Hospital. Some patients in the hospital got tired of hospital food and I, for a small transportation fee, would get them what they wanted at the hamburger place. If I remember correctly, the cost of a hamburger, fries and a shake was forty cents.

I spent most of my time on Piedmont Avenue in a small library located on 41st Street right across the train station. This library was the closest branch to the house. It was a small Spanish-style building that fit the mood of the Avenue: unobtrusive, quaint, heavily used and quiet. I used to go to the stacks and sit down and read for hours. During the school year I sometimes would do my homework there. I got to know the librarian quite well. The librarian was a tall plain-looking woman who wore glasses, always wore her dark brown hair in a bun at her neck, seemed to always wear a skirt, a white blouse and a dark sweater, and spoke with a voice that was barely audible even if you spoke to her inside the building. She was always kind to me and always helped me when I had a question or needed to find a reference.

But late one evening, I think I let her down when she came to me for help. I was reading in the stacks when she came and asked me what she should do about a drunk who was sitting at one of the tables. I got up and saw the man sitting quietly at a table apparently reading a magazine. He was not doing anything to disrupt the library; the librarian and I were the only other people in the place. But he did, much to my consternation, wet his thumb with his tongue before noisily turning the pages of the magazine. I did not think there was any reason to be concerned, and so I told her, "Nothing." It was obvious to me from the look on her face that she did not like my answer. I returned to the stacks and shortly after I heard the man being ejected by a policeman that the librarian had summoned. The drunk was now loud, belligerent and fighting the ejection from the library. He swore and yelled at the officer that he was not doing anything wrong, and he caused such a racket that people gathered outside the library to look at the scene. The librarian stood behind her desk looking flustered and unsure of what to do. It was minutes before the policeman quieted the man and convinced him to leave the area before silence returned to the street outside the library. I returned to the stacks to read. Afterwards, whenever I returned to the library, I noticed that the librarian's attitude towards me was polite but decidedly cool.

If one follows Piedmont Avenue north until it ends, one will run into The Chapel of the Chimes, Saint Mary's, Mountain View and the Jewish cemeteries. These cemeteries overlooked the lake and quarry that Al, my brother, and I used to play in. Uncle Fred Grecia, who brought Mom from the Philippines to the States, is buried in Mountain View cemetery. My father Antonio Judan Mendoza, who I did not know (he died when I was four years old), and my stepfather, Flaviano Apilado Jucutan, who I barely knew even though he was my father figure for thirty five years, are both buried in Saint Mary's cemetery. One day I visited these graves and wondered what might have been if Daddy had not died, if we were raised closer to our Filipino roots, if we were raised in another area of Oakland. If, if, if. I thought about Mom, my brothers and sisters, my own family and some of the events that put me here today and what might have transpired...if. I had a hard time concentrating on these unanswerable questions for the day was clear and bright and the view from the cemetery of the Bay Area was absolutely beautiful. It was so clear that one could count the individual buildings in San Francisco and see the flash of windows on the cars as they crossed the Bay Bridge. I chided myself on my foolishness and as I walked back to the car I thought that despite my death or, death in the family, life will go on, the family will go on, and that is the way it should be. Dwelling on what might have been was a useless expense better put away until one is very old and very wise. At that time, one could use such questions as a mental exercise to perhaps try and prove to oneself that God seems to play dice with people's lives and that if anything, he does indeed seem to have a sense of humor. As I left the cemeteries I was content to know that my father, my stepfather and my granduncle still live on in my memory.

200 GRAND AVENUE

Eleanor M. Hipol Luis

The Veterans Building, 200 Grand Avenue, was a simple structure among tall apartment buildings, located across Lake Merritt just outside downtown Oakland. From the mid-1950's through the 1960's, we frequented the building in the evening when spotlights highlighted the french pane glass doors that opened to a large terrace along the west side of the building. Here you could stand and look over Lake Merritt glistening under the street lights in the darkness of the night. It was a facility that housed a majority of the events sponsored by Filipino community organizations, especially the organizations affiliated with the

American Legion. This was where the family members of American Legion Rizal Post 598 of Oakland spent one Saturday every month, and celebrated holidays, held annual events, fundraisers and other activities. For our family, membership in this organization brought us into a social circle within a Filipino community where new friendships were developed.

The American Legion Rizal Post 598 was organized for veterans, comrades as they were called, who served in the armed services during World War II and the Korean War. During World War II the Filipino men in the U.S. who enlisted in the Army were soldiers in the 1st and 2nd Filipino Infantry Regiments assigned to serve overseas in Guam, New Guinea and the Philippines. For many of the soldiers it was their first trip to their homeland after a decade or two. Some soldiers married Pinays from the Visayas in the Philippines where the soldiers were stationed. Upon their return to the U.S. they immediately prepared for the passage of their new bride and, maybe even their new family to join them in America.

My father came to the U.S. in 1926, leaving his homeland to look for the money that, he was told, grew on trees. The story was a lie. He enlisted in the Army during World War II to receive an automatic U.S. citizenship. After the war he returned to the U.S. as a single man who would wait for his bride-to-be to join him in Oakland where he resided prior to his overseas tour. He received his honorable discharge from the Army and shortly after became a member of the Rizal Post 598. The Women's Auxiliary Rizal Unit 598 was organized by and for the wives of the members of the Rizal Post, and in the 1950's, the Sons of the American Legion

Rizal Post 598 and Junior Auxiliary were organized for their sons and daughters.

Babysitters were an unknown commodity back then and if you didn't have a sibling old enough to care for you at home, your parents brought you everywhere they went. So, once a month I found myself at these Saturday night Rizal Post and Auxiliary meetings at the Vet's Building. But I didn't mind because I knew other kids would be there and this meant "playtime." Our attention span at these meetings lasted through the opening ceremonies when we actively participated.

The children of the Rizal Post and Auxiliary were always asked to perform for the adults. This made our parents proud. During one of the Auxiliary's monthly meetings, I was asked to recite the poem, "In Flanders Fields." I felt awkward because I understood the poem to be about veterans who had died. Despite this feeling, I recited the poem. On the night of my recital, I was dressed in full uniform: navy blue skirt, white blouse, hair freshly permed, and navy blue auxiliary hat on my head. I was a midget Navy Wave. When called to recite the poem, I spoke so fast that I know no one understood what I said. But it didn't matter because after this deed, I felt that I had committed myself to "something," although it never became clear what that "something" was.

As a child, I didn't realize how much of an impact the military made on these veterans. I never thought about the reasons the Rizal Post was organized nor did I link a "war" to the members in the organization. Back then I lived a child's "play" world and a "war" was a scene in a movie shown on television or on a theater screen. It was only when I took the time to watch the members of the Rizal Post that I noticed how these men saluted their adjutant or executed an about face with pride and dignity, and we children emulated their actions as best as we could.

Each meeting opened with everyone standing and saluting the flag as it was being posted by the marshal and sergeant-at-arms. We recited the "Pledge of Allegiance" and sang the "Star Spangled Banner." Then we recited the American Legion preamble, some of which I memorized, "....for God and country we associate ourselves together for the following purposes, to uphold and defend the Constitution of the United States of America. To maintain law and order, to foster and perpetuate a one hundred percent Americanism..." After these lines, without the "little card," I was lost. We remained standing and bowed our heads for the opening prayer given by the Chaplain, then the official dialogue between the officers began.

The Vet's Building was enormous and we investigated all the rooms from the second floor to the basement and we made up games along the way. We knew just how long to stay in an area, timing our move with the facilities manager, Stan, who was always walking through the building. Sometimes we took off our shoes and slid on the dark ceramic tiles that covered the hallways of the first and second floors and if the grand ballroom was open, our game of run and slide on the waxed hardwood floor was even more fun.

On Veteran's Day, the members of the Rizal Post and Auxiliary, along with the Sons and Juniors, marched in local parades starting in a downtown area and ending at a cemetery (usually in Oakland). At the cemetery we placed miniature American flags at the headstones of the veterans' graves, making sure not to step on any of the dead in the process.

To celebrate Mother's and Father's Day, a picnic was usually held at Hayward Plunge, one of the biggest and, at the time, nicest parks in the East Bay. There was a large picnic area on a hillside located away from the main street and public activities, complete with barbecue grills and tables with benches and a large grassy area where you could lounge comfortably. There were public tennis courts and an Olympic-size indoor swimming pool which was one of the only public pools in this area. At the picnic the old and the young played games such as tug-of-war, relay, and sack races and the winners of these games won prizes. The tug-of-war games were always fun because there were several possible combinations. It pitted the men against the women, the old against the young, the boys against the girls, women and girls against the men and boys, families against families, and the losers always fell flat on their butts. There was always lots of food and beverages and a cake decorated to fit the occasion to be shared among all of the attendees. Events like this gave us children a chance to see our parents in a different light. We saw them move out of their roles as moms and dads and be kids; they were actually playing with us and with each other, jumping, falling, rolling on the ground and our laughter echoed in the park.

As the years went by, and the Sons and Juniors became teenagers, our parents looked into other activities for our involvement. A Filipina dance group was formed under the direction of one of the mothers in the Auxiliary. She was tiny in stature, had a stern voice and seemed unapproachable. She was a replica of our own moms so we weren't as intimidated as we might have been whenever she yelled at us for not paying attention or for fooling around. She was the one who accepted the task of teaching our large group, ages 12-18, which was quite a feat especially with our "teenage" attitudes. Despite all my moaning and groaning, I thank her for teaching me some of the dances of the Philippine culture.

The Sons and Juniors continued to march in the Veteran's Day parades but with a new flair. We became a marching drum corps complete with a drum major, drummers and majorettes. The custom-made uniforms worn by the majorettes included a white and silver long sleeved jacket, a white sleeveless satin top with "shimmy" fringe at the waist, a short blue pleated satin skirt, and clunky white leather marching boots with a tassel hanging on the center front of the boot. The members of the drum corps wore loose blue pants, a gold long loose sleeved button down shirt, and a blue cap. The drum major looked very impressive dressed in a blue satin uniform complete with the headgear and the leader's baton. We were taught to march, drum and twirl a baton by only the best, the Weldonians. The award winning Weldonians were known for their marching finesse, baton twirling and precision drumming and their attitude. We weren't really interested in parade competition, which was a big part of the Weldonian attitude, and the lessons were costly, so this activity wasn't one that lasted very long.

The Vet's Building was within walking distance of Broadway Bowl, the local bowling alley that served as the meeting place for many of the teenagers from Oakland and outlying cities. One Saturday, while our parents were attending their monthly meeting, a few of us decided to go bowling, so we walked to Broadway Bowl. Bowling was fun but expensive. The pin ball machines only cost twenty-five cents so we played these machines, all the while crossing our fingers that we would be spared the embarrassment of not being able to show proof that we were old enough (18 years old) to play the machines.

At Broadway Bowl we met and became familiar with others who frequented the bowling alley. In fact we became so comfortable there that on one of these nights we forgot about the time and stayed past the hour for us to leave. We rushed back to the Vet's Building only to find that the meetings ended earlier than usual and my parents were impatiently waiting for me. It was at this point that my parents decided that I should stay home while they attend the meetings and that was the end of me having to tag along with my parents. I was okay with this, but still found myself at the Vet's Building for the Rizal Post and Auxiliary dances.

The New Year's Eve Ball was the biggest fundraising event sponsored by the Rizal Post and Auxiliary. From the 1950's through the 1960's, this dance continued to draw relatives and friends as well as people from the Filipino communities of the Bay Area. In the mid-60's the Miss American Legion queen contest was held and this became the highlight of the New Year's Eve Ball.

I remember this one particular New Year's Eve Ball held in the late 1960's. It seemed as if the musicians were the same as those that were hired to play at the dance when I was eight. The combo was composed of Filipino musicians whose instruments included drums, piano, upright bass, saxophone, trumpet and one of the musicians doubled up on vocals. They played songs from the hit parade during the war (late 1940's), some rock 'n roll from the 1950's, and of course, the ever popular TWIST.

There we were as teenagers (after almost a decade) dancing next to our parents at this New Year's Ball. We danced slow to the waltz, added extra footwork to the cha-cha, mastered the swing, and ignored the tango. I was still fond of the song, *Cherry Pink and Apple Blossom White,* and still enjoyed watching my parents dance the waltz to *Around the World in Eighty Days.*

"Social boxes" were popular at community dances. This was a special dance where several young ladies, chosen from among the guests, served as participants. Each one had a canvasser who would entice people to pay to dance with the lady. There was usually a $2.00 donation but some gave more. The main objective was for the canvasser to keep the lady on the dance floor to make as much money as possible within a certain time frame. The funds collected went to the organization. The participant who collected the most money received a surprise gift. There were several social boxes held during the evening and each time they would be finished, the master of ceremonies would announce the winner and in a thick Filipino accent command, "Ebreybudy danse!"

No New Year's Eve dance would be complete without an incident or a fight or two and at this particular dance there would be no exception. It began when a smoke bomb went off and a member of the Rizal Post, without any proof whatsoever, began accusing an innocent teenage male for setting off the smoke bomb. The father of the accused teenager (also a member of the Post) entered the scene and the two adults exchanged words in Ilocano (one of the dialects spoken in the Philippines). The tone of the language was such that one knew, without understanding a word, that it wasn't a friendly conversation, and a crowd began to gather around the two who were arguing. The wives of the two men interjected and successfully removed the men from the scene.

Next, two teens got into a verbal altercation and as their older brothers tried to intervene, the brothers ended up in a fist fight. The cause of the fight was one of those boy-girl situations (provoked by jealousy) where one guy was seen outside at the bridge (lover's lane) with a young lady that the other guy liked, only she never knew he liked her. But that didn't matter, the fight went on. This fight produced a "domino effect," starting at one side of the room and continuing to the opposite end. The elders who tried to break up the fight began fighting among themselves. It looked as if everyone in this grand ballroom (capacity 200+) was fighting. Chairs were flying and people were running in all directions. Kids were crying and women were screaming at their husbands, trying to grab hold of their clothing to keep him from joining in the fight. Dads were swinging and swearing, "Gaud dam son-a-mabits," while wives were yelling, "Dat's enup now, da-dee, stop dat now, please!"

The security guards were of no use; this was too much for only two officers to handle. Someone was stabbed, but the wound was superficial and the victim was able to walk out on his own. The police were summoned to the scene, but arrived as the crowd exited the building. That was a night to remember; a little more action at this dance than at the others. The band usually played until 1:00 a.m., but if I remember correctly, this New Year's Eve Ball ended before midnight.

As I think back, many of us Juniors and Sons spent a decade or more attending meetings, activities and events sponsored by the American Legion Rizal Post 598 and Auxiliary held at the Vet's Building. I grew out of my teens and went into yet another metamorphosis, and after I heard about those members who made their transitions, I began to think about what this organization meant to them and to me.

I realized that the American Legion Rizal Post 598 was more than a social organization. To its members, it was a brotherhood pact that bonded those who fought for their two countries during World War II – the U.S. and the Philippines. It was a bond for those who were living in the States without their families and it gave them a sense of belonging. It gave the Filipino veteran yet another reason for being recognized as an 'American,' as well as boosting their Filipino pride. They became more determined to be recognized, despite difficulties they endured. For the veteran, the meetings were more than just a Saturday evening "get together." It was a way of healing the physical, psychological and spiritual war wounds with those who had the same experiences and feelings.

As with any organization, it had its quirks and the members their trivial disagreements and bruised egos. But for the most part, the members developed a new Filipino community and brought their families into this community. For their wives and their offspring, this Unit became their extended family. Together they reserved their place in the history of Filipinos in America.

I extend a sincere "Thank you!" to the Rizal Post 598 veterans, Uncles who came back to the States and continued to build for us. "Thank you!" to the Aunties of the Auxiliary who incorporated the family into Unit 598, and to the Juniors and Sons "Thanks for the memories!" I hope that if and when we get the chance, we take the time to drive by the Vet's Building, and that we think about our history, our family, our friends and that we keep the memories alive by sharing them with our families.

Rizal, Jose, national hero of the Philippines

Pinay, feminine variation of *Pinoy,* an adaptation of 'Filipino'

ADOBO, TAMALES, BLUES, & JAZZ
ON MAGNOLIA STREET

Evangeline Canonizado Buell

When I was a young girl, I lived in West Oakland, a neighborhood filled with immigrant families from Mexico, China, Japan, Portugal, and Italy. There was a sprinkling of Greeks, Spanish Basque, and Czechoslovakians and two Filipino families. During WWII many Afro-Americans from the south came to live and work in the nearby shipyards. We were one of the two Filipino families living in our neighborhood, a rarity at that time.

We lived on Magnolia Street which was lined with Victorian houses. Our home had three bedrooms, two full bathrooms, a big kitchen with an adjoining sun porch and a large dining room. There was a full basement underneath, where we could hang clothes to dry during rainy weather, play games, and store food and household goods.

Our house faced the West overlooking the San Francisco Bay Bridge, and on a clear day we could see the mouth of the Golden Gate bridge and watch the boats slipping in and out to sea. When the fog trailed over the ocean and through the bay to our house, we could hear the fog horn bellowing through the murky mist guiding the ships and boats safely into nearby ports.

The Key System train whistled and tooted its horn as it stopped at the corner to scoop up passengers to take them to San Francisco, and during the 1939 World's Fair stopped at Treasure Island to let hundreds of people off to attend the festivities.

Before the San Francisco Bay Bridge was built, ferry boats were the means for transportation across the bay. As I stood on the deck, I loved to smell and feel the spray of the salt water, the fog as it enfolded me, the wind tossing my long hair, and swirling all around me, forging the swaying boat toward the towering ferry terminal building. On a clear night the lights of San Francisco shimmered like tiny jewels. In the near distance, the little bayside towns of Sausalito, Tiburon and Belvedere along with Angel Island beckoned us with their welcoming fluttering sparkles of light.

From our house, we could walk a few blocks to the Oakland Main Library, and Cole Elementary School was just around the corner. Chinatown, close by, was always teeming with people of all ages, and at all hours of the day and evening. We did most of our grocery shopping there because ingredients for cooking Philippine food was available to us. Our weekly shopping forays were an exciting array of sights, sounds and smells. We were enclosed by narrow streets, surrounded by small open shops displaying fresh produce fruit, and fish, extending on to the sidewalks for easy access. The aroma of dim sum (steamed dumplings), rice cakes, roasting pigs, ducks, and chicken filled our nostrils, sometimes our hungry stomachs when we stopped for lunch or dinner. For just a nickel we were treated to a large round char sieu bow (steamed barbecued pork bun) plucked piping hot from steam baskets. Famished, we munched happily as we wended our way through the crowd of people to the abundantly stocked market stalls to buy our weekly groceries.

The street trolley was the main transportation to get around town to the large department stores - Hales, Kahn's, JC Penney's - shops, movies, and restaurants. It was so exciting jumping on and off the streetcars, hearing the clanging bells and whirring sounds of the wheels against the tracks. The city seemed to celebrate our special outings with cars honking their horns, trolley cars gliding along their tracks clackety clack, hundreds of people bustling to and fro, their voices one big sound of fragmented conversations, police directing traffic and the wailing hooting horn of the Southern Pacific train zipping through the city. It was a happy chorus of blended sounds.

Then WWII broke out, and I remember having to wear a large button that said, "I am a loyal American Filipino" in bright red, white, and blue. We could not leave home without it. Grandma worried about us especially when we would forget our buttons. She had several for us to wear on our various jackets and sweaters. At that time people could not

143

tell one Asian from another, and we were sometimes mistaken for Japanese. Our Japanese friends and neighbors had been taken away to internment camps. Our family was shaken by the traumatic experience of seeing them leave. They were lined up to board buses across the street from our house. We bade them farewell, hugging and crying. Grandma was grief stricken for a long time. One day I did the inevitable. I left home without my button to go shopping downtown. The grocery clerk called me "jap" and told me I could not buy rice, and another sold me some inferior rice. I felt humiliated wearing the button and when I didn't I was discriminated against.

Still, in spite of the war, which brought on many air raids and black outs, I remember evening walks through our neighborhood at dinner time. One could smell the variety of cooking coming from the different houses. The mixture of delicious odors wafted through the block overwhelming us with pangs of hunger: ham hocks and greens, fried chicken, simmering spaghetti sauce, whiffs of garlic and onions sauteeing, bread, pies, and baklava baking in the ovens. Blending in, tamales and tortillas filled the air. The lingering odor of crushed grapes from the Italian wine maker next door, the cooking of chicken adobo from our house, mingled in with the Portuguese linguisa from across the street. Pots, pans, and dishes rattled along with moms and dads calling their children to come in and eat. "Dinner is ready."

In the summer months, the Carnation Creamery was a colorful noisy scene of long lines of neighborhood children waiting to buy the giant ice cream cones. My sister Rosita, cousin Rosario, and I eagerly waited our turn among them, clutching a dime in our fists to pay for the double scoop cones of strawberry and chocolate. Hot fudge and caramel sundaes with whipped cream and nuts featured at the Soda Fountain was a weekly treat for us.

Up the block the Nabisco Shredded Wheat Factory a ten story building rose into the sky with railroad tracks entering through a tunnel on the ground floor. It dominated the place towering majestically above the neighborhood and could be seen for miles. At times the intense odor of fiery roasted cereal congested the air.

The beauty and warmth of the music of Mexico, China, Japan, Italy, Greece, and Portugal surrounded me. There was gospel, spirituals, rhythm and blues, southern ballads, jazz, Mariachi, as well as my own ethnic songs and dances of the Philippines.

This was West Oakland in the 1940's.

THE MODERN POOL HALL

Joseph T. Arriola

Some of the earliest memories of my childhood take place in the Modern Pool Hall, the establishment that Louie (Loye) Saraquino, owned and ran. Before walking through the door of the pool hall I would often peer through the glass and oak framed door. The door was old and massive, too heavy for me to open without my father.

As my father loomed above me readying himself to open the door, I would place my hands on the glass, while adjusting my head forward to look in. The first thing I would see was the hustle and bustle of the activity within. Cigar and cigarette smoke reeked the air. I could see patches of light peering from the sunroof in the center of the room. Heavy wisps of cloudlike smoke that traveled throughout filtered the sunlight at various angles.

Once my father had wrenched open the mammoth door I would squeeze beneath him entering the pool hall. A cacophony of sounds would immediately invade my senses, bursts of laughter and profane language, the shuffling of cards, and the smacking of wooden sticks into pool balls.

I was three years old when I first set foot inside the Modern Pool Hall. Dressed in holster and sixgun, boots, badge and cowboy hat, the men that frequented the Modern Pool Hall, knew me as Jo Jo the Marshal. I liked going with my father to see Loye and the unique assortment of characters that would come in and out of Loye's Modern Pool Hall. I wouldn't learn until much later that the ebb and flow of faces depended on the seasons of the year. Not until I was thirteen and myself a farm laborer would I understand that these men had come from the Philippines, then a colony of the United States, to work as migrant field workers.

"Marshal, good aptearnoon," a friend of my father would say as he greeted me and my father on his way out the door. "Jo Jo, where is your 'orse," another man might say while stepping over to the counter to buy a Toscani cigar. Each friend of my father would say hello to me as if I was one of the "boys." Little did I realize that I was a rarity.

Few Pilipinas, women from the home country, made the journey to the land of opportunity. And because of racial policies, and anti-miscegenation laws, preventing Pilipinos from marrying outside of their race, few of the men that frequented the Modern Pool Hall had even been married much less had children. Little did I realize that I and the other children like me would be the only family that many of these men would ever know.

Immediately to the left, was a long glass and oak stained counter. It was from there that Loye conducted the business of the Modern Pool Hall.. Loye collected money from the card and the pool players, and sold potato chips, sodas and candy bars from behind the counter.

"Now, Jo Jo, you are going to be good today," Loye would say in his stateliest of manners while standing behind the counter. Loye spoke English in a very clear and elegant manner. His English was unbroken. Unlike his patrons Loye was a formal man. He rarely wore a hat. But, he always wore a lightweight, shark skin suit, albeit without a tie.

In later years, I would discover that Loye was different not just because he was a businessman, but because he was a worldly man. Loye had come to the "land of opportunity" to seek an education, to be successful. Unlike many of the others, who came simply for the promise of work Loye came to the United States to live a dream. But economic and racial injustices would prevent him from living his dream. He would never attain an education and he would never become an engineer. In later years, I would discover that the dreams of some men are meant only to be dreamed by one and accomplished by another.

"Don't worry, Loye, I promise I'll be good," I stated with sincerity. "I promise I'll be a good boy," I continued. "Very good," he replied.

Loye kept the money in a metal cash register that looked like an old style typewriter with keys that when pressed would elicit the sound of ching-ching. The cash register was so ancient that it had to have been manufactured in the late 1800's.

However, to my delight the counter presented small rectangular grey boxes wrapped in cellophane, filled with Ludger's cherry drops, Baby Ruth candy bars and, best of all, the "cowboy," a single candy bar made up of chewy caramel and coconut bits.

Just beyond the counter, in a place of honor sat a magnificent pool table. The table was made of the finest oak. Six leather pockets one at each corner and two at equidistant points on the long sides of the table. On top this table was a sea of kelly green felt. Oftentimes I would want to touch the smooth felt on the table and crash the balls against each other. But, Loye made it clear that the table was off limits.

The single fluorescent tube that hung above the table accentuated the brisk green felt while shading the lacquered wood. On the wall, was a rack holding seven pool cues of various weights and lengths. A second rack made specifically for placing the balls that were to be pocketed was framed to the right of the cue rack. Just below both racks sat a long wooden bench

When I was old enough to look down upon the pool table rather than peering up and across it, and when I was allowed to shoot pool on the table rather than simply watch from the bench, I would learn well the angles of that table, the physics involved when two objects collide and the mathematics I would need to know to collect my wagers.

When in the summer the lettuce was ripe for harvest, the Modern Pool Hall became alive with activity. This would be Loye's busiest time of the year. With the money he made from the Modern Pool Hall he would send to his brother's son. And some day, his nephew would come to America. Someday, his nephew would attain an education and become an engineer.

The boys, men like Andres, Boston Blackie, and Robert the Loverboy, would return from such places as the fish canneries in Alaska, the deserts of Yuma, Arizona, and the asparagus fields of the San Joaquin Valley.

Andres was a tough old man who had been in many scrapes. Oftentimes, I would want to keep my distance from him. I would want to avoid the stench of whiskey that was usually on his breath. Yet, he was a loyal friend to my parents, and when we later ran our own pool hall he guarded the place with the gun that was beneath his pillow. Boston Blackie was a boxer in the early 1920's, and was my godfather. Robert, was a light-skinned Pilipino with almond eyes and black hair combed back with the sweet scent of Dixie Peach pomade. As his name suggested, he was a lover.

"Jo Jo, kome 'ere," yelled my Ninong (godfather) Boston Blackie in his high pitched voice. "Ninong," I shouted as I ran toward him. Abruptly, he put his hands into a boxing posture and said "You pight me?" I stopped dead in my tracks. My hands instinctively going into a defensive posture. "OK, Ninong, let's fight," when out of nowhere a slow looping left hook would circle my head. I would duck too late and Boston Blackie would say "Bery goud. Bery goud," as he scooped me up and carried me to the counter.

"Jo Jo, opin yore hawnd," Boston Blackie would say with a smile on his face. My eyes would widen as I stretched out my hand eagerly for my present. A shiny quarter. Two-bits to spend on anything I wanted.

"Thank you, Ninong, thank you." I would say as he lowered me to the floor and I scurried to the counter.

The entire floor of the Modern Pool Hall was made of hardwood. Loye would sprinkle saw dust on the floors every morning and then would sweep it up each night. Strangely, there had been only one pool table in the Modern Pool Hall while an array of six round card tables placed in an L-shaped configuration dominated the rest of the building. Besides the ash trays that sat on the tables there would usually be a coffee can that acted as a makeshift spittoon. Such coffee cans usually sat below the tables. I later figured out that if one of the card players missed in his aim for the coffee can, the saw dust on the floor would absorb the mess.

"Tata (uncle) Andres, why do you spit all the time?" I asked as Andres sat at the card table, caressing his cards, while slowly opening them for analysis. *"Lintick na* (damn it)! "he exclaimed in disgust as he threw down his cards. "Tata Andres, why do you spit?" I again asked out of intense curiosity, standing patiently with one hand on the back of Andres' chair and the other hand holding vertically my cowboy candy bar positioning it for my next bite. He turned toward me, in semi-shock. His mind so intensely concerned with the game had been diverted to my attention.

If Loye had been watching I am sure that he would have said that I had broken my promise, that I was now being a bad boy. But, Loye was behind the counter helping a customer, so I knew that I could ask all the important questions that I wanted.

Andres looked at me quizzically and smiled. I could see the glint of his teeth dulled and brownish in color with bits of stuff on it. "Tobacco," he replied as he turned back to the table and spit some more black stuff into a coffee can.

In truth, the Modern Pool Hall wasn't simply a pool hall. It was *sugalan* a gambling house. But really it was a men's club, a place where they could exhibit their skills on the pool table, a place where they could *sugal*, gamble for the big stakes.

The most common games of chance included a type of rummy played with two decks of cards, and mostro, a type of three-man solitaire using eleven decks of cards. After each round of cards, a quarter was collected from each player and placed into a cigar box, the money was designated as house commission.

But by far the most intriguing game, the game that involved the highest stakes, was Pi Qu, a game of Chinese origin using domino type tiles. It was the game that was the most colorful to see, hear and feel. The dealer would mix the dominos face down, clacking them, from various angles as he rubbed the back of the tiles with both of his hands moving in circular motions. He would then stack them four at a time and then stack the stacks along side each other, clacking the tiles with every motion. The players would all be watching, waiting in anticipation. A pair of dice would be thrown and depending upon the numbers, each player would receive his stack of four tiles.

Strangely, it was the only game where the dealer and all the players stood beside the table rather than sitting at it. I never really understood why this was so. Yet, I did know that this was the one table where the players either yelled and screamed in seeming ecstasy or left the table in silenced anger. It was the one table where in a single night, a man could lose a week's wages.

Like the pool table, the Pi Qu table was another place that I wasn't allowed to approach too close. Robert the Loverboy stormed away from the Pi Qu table in rage. He didn't see me standing there two feet behind him. He had almost knocked me into the floor as he pulled away from the table. Luckily, he was able to grab me before I hit the ground. I had never seen Loverboy so mad. For that moment everyone seemed to notice what had happened.

"What's wrong? What's wrong, Loverboy?" I said with concern. I could hear someone whisper he lost "pive hundrid." But, Loverboy did-n't answer me. He instead continued to walk away. "Loverboy!" I again shouted.

I hadn't noticed that Loye was standing nearby. He had witnessed the entire altercation. "Jo Jo what did I tell you," Loye said softly but in a stern manner. "Honest Loye, I was far from the table," I said meaning it.

"Jo Jo it's time to go," my father said as he grasped my hand, saving me from Loye's wrath. I can still see my father and I walking out of the Modern Pool Hall. I turn my head back, continuing to be led by my father. I raise my hand guiltily and wave goodbye to Loye. Loye is still standing erect watching us as we leave the Modern Pool Hall.

It's gone now. It is but an empty building, a shell filled with dust and old furniture. Its doors are padlocked. It is but a memory from a child's dream. Its inhabitants, they are but ghosts, ghosts that linger only in my memories. But from its dreams nephews were able to come to the land of opportunity to attain education and to become engineers and little boys wearing cowboy hats became real lawmen.

There will always be an aliveness, in the Modern Pool Hall, a crackling of electricity that I have never felt again. The Modern Pool Hall was my Disneyland, sitting on the wooden benches, swishing the saw dust in swirls between my feet, watching the pool players glide across a sea of green felt and rainbow covered balls.

I will remember Loye, Andres, Boston Blackie, Robert the Loverboy and the other colorful men from the Modern Pool Hall, for their laughter, and for their stories of travel and adventure. But I will always love them, for the invariable "two-bits" they would give to me to buy "cowboy" candy bars.

---

tata, tatay, father or an elder of your father's age who may or may not be blood related, e.g. an uncle, a community elder

THE OLD MAN

Tony Robles

The old man would sometimes say
     Man, don't you know we the niggahs
     of the orient?

Then he'd start working on his rice
     and adobo and chili and tomatoes

Man, you better eat all that food on your plate
he'd say to me

Then he'd talk about all the people
     starvin' in China

And how lucky I was to be eating
     and even luckier to be breathing

He'd sweat a lot while eating
     it was like work

Only difference being
     that he enjoyed it

Scooping the rice with his hand
     and mixing it with the adobo

What'd you learn in school today?

Nuthin'

You better study hard in school
Ain't no one gonna give you nothin' for free

You wanna clean toilets like me
     all your life?

You want a job where you can sit down

Which brings us to today
        where I'm sitting on the toilet and writing
This, when I should be sitting at my desk and working

Grandma would put fish on my plate

Fish is brain food, kid

Get your education
        that is something they can never take away
        from you

Then my dad would be silent
        eating with his hands

I'd have my fork, picking slowly

And he'd finally speak

You know there's people starvin' in China?

UNCLE EDDIE'S RESTAURANT

Benjamin Mendoza

Oakland was a workingman's town. It did not have the cosmopolitan atmosphere that San Francisco had. It was a town filled with small businesses and factories and government bases where people worked. The people lived in the different districts of the city. I was born and raised in the Temescal District. As a rule of thumb, the workers lived on the flat lands of Oakland while the gentry populated the hill areas. In the late 1940's it was a city that was about to undergo a transformation that would forever change its character. But that transformation was still a few years in the future.

However, two events were taking place in the city that could not be ignored. One was the replacement of the streetcars with buses. The other was an upcoming City election that was to be hotly contested. The reform movement campaigned that the city should become a modern city by closing all gambling places and houses of prostitution that they said gave a city a bad name, was bad for the youth and tarnished the image of the business community.

It was during this time that my Uncle Eddie offered me a job in his restaurant in the Chinatown area of Oakland. The main Chinatown business area was located between Franklin and Harrison streets and between Sixth and Tenth streets. Here were to be found many grocery stores, restaurants, barber shops, meat, fish and poultry businesses and dry goods stores. Many people and families lived in Chinatown in the many flats above businesses and in the many residence hotels. The area always seemed to teem with people during the day and at night. My Uncle, a few years after he was discharged from the Army, began his restaurant here. The restaurant was located on the northern edge of Chinatown, on Tenth Street. The building was very narrow. A window proclaimed "Eddie's Restaurant" but the only thing that could be seen from the outside was the cash register that sat next to the window. On the left as you entered the restaurant was a counter and stools. The only way back to the kitchen area was to walk to the end of the counter. When one reached the end of the counter, one saw a closed door straight ahead and a small aisle that led left to the kitchen and serving area.

The restaurant served Filipino foods. The menu included *adobo, pansit,* and *pinakbet* whose vegetables consisted mostly of bitter melon. One could also order coffee, tea and soft drinks. I was hired as a dishwasher, cleaner and gofer. When business got busy I was also to be an order taker and server. The only restriction that my Uncle put on me was that under no circumstances was I ever to enter the back room. I can still see my Uncle speaking in his loud voice, wagging his finger at me and pointing to the forbidden door. I was to work on Friday and Saturday evenings. I began working on a Friday and was expecting that the evening would be busy, but to my surprise there was only moderate business. Many customers who entered the restaurant would only order a cup of coffee, talk to my Uncle in *Ilocano* for awhile, and then disappear into the back room. During the course of the evening I heard the clicking and clacking of tiles whenever the back room door opened and guessed what action was taking place behind the back room door. I said nothing to my Uncle about my hunch and finished my first day on the job.

I believe that it was the second Saturday that I worked that I found, during one of my cleaning rounds, the two buttons underneath the counter where the cash register was situated. My Uncle was out shopping and there was no one in the restaurant. I pushed one of the buttons and heard a buzzer sound in the back room. The second button I pushed produced a 'click' at the back door. Looking through the window for my Uncle and not seeing him, I rushed to the back door and found it open. Upon entering I saw in the light streaming through the open door three or four half-moon tables with stools around each table. The table closest to me had in the middle of the top, the outline of rectangles that followed the contour of the table. All the tables were covered with a green cloth. I guessed that Blackjack and Pai Gow were played on the tables. The clacking noise came from the tiles used in Pai Gow. I took a last look and then closed the door and hurried to the front of the restaurant. I knew that if my Uncle ever found out what I had done he would have given me a tongue-lashing before he fired me. This I would have regretted since I needed the money and it was very difficult for Filipino youths to get a job.

One day, having washed all the dishes and cleaned the stainless steel sink, I was topping off the salt and peppershakers on the counter when I noticed that a car had pulled in front of the restaurant. My Uncle had just gone into the back room. It wasn't until the men started to get out of the car that I realized that they were Oakland policemen. I ran to the cash register and was about to press the buzzer button when my Uncle yelled from the back door to leave it alone and for me to start cooking rice in the large pot. The two policemen entered the restaurant and greeted my Uncle. My Uncle returned the greeting and asked the officers about their respective families. In the meantime I had measured out eight cups of rice and was washing it in the sink. I heard the cash register bell ring and out of the corner of my eyes I saw my Uncle raise the money tray and pull out two envelopes. He gave one to each of the officers saying "just a little something for the family for the holidays." One of the officers said, "Thanks Eddie. Hope you have a great Christmas." With that both officers left.

No one had to explain to me what was in the envelopes. What I wanted to know and did not dare ask my Uncle was how much was in the envelopes? My Uncle never explained his actions to me and our conversation was limited to what was going on with the restaurant. A few months later my Uncle gave me a list of groceries to buy at the Tai Wah grocery store on Eighth Street. He added that I was not to return to the restaurant for an hour. He emphasized this by having me repeat what he had just said. By this time I was used to working for my Uncle and did not ask for an explanation for his unusual instructions. Even taking my time I was finished with this shopping chore in twenty minutes. I carried the shopping bags to a point on Webster Street where I could just see the restaurant. From here I looked up at the Oakland Tribune Tower clock and saw that I still had thirty-five minutes before I could return to the restaurant.

I was wondering where I could kill the time when I heard police sirens coming up Tenth Street. Three police cars stopped in front of the restaurant and six police officers got out of the police cars and entered the restaurant. From my vantage point less than a block from the restaurant I heard loud voices and noises that sounded like furniture being roughly moved. A few people walked by and peered into the restaurant window but most just kept walking seemingly oblivious to what was happening. About fifteen minutes later I saw the police and my Uncle exit the front door. On the sidewalk my Uncle and the police continued their conversation for a few minutes before the police left. My Uncle was left standing in front of the restaurant speaking to passers-by. I waited another five minutes and returned to the restaurant. My Uncle was wiping down the counter when I entered. All he said to me was to put away the groceries and get ready for the evening dinner customers. He never mentioned the incident that I had just witnessed. Many years later I learned that I had witnessed a routine police raid. Someone in the police department always notified the individuals before a raid. This way nothing illegal was ever found on the premises that was raided.

What did I think of this unusual situation that I found myself? About the only thing I thought about was that it was a job and that I was earning badly needed money. I do not think that I ever considered the moral issues. After all, most fourteen-year-olds have one-track minds and if put to the test, an average fourteen-year-old would probably choose monetary issues over any moral consideration. Oakland was a very safe city during the 1940's and early 1950's. Many times I would leave the restaurant very late at night. Instead of taking the bus home, I would sometimes walk from the restaurant on Tenth Street to home on Shafter near Thirty-eighth Street. In the downtown area there were many couples "window shopping" at all hours of the evening. Many of the police calls were for public drunkenness. There was never a time that I can remember when I was growing up that I was afraid of walking the streets of Oakland at night.

My Uncle's gambling establishment was just one of many in the Chinatown area of Oakland. In this same downtown area and continuing to the Estuary there were houses of prostitution and places where people could fence stolen material. The longer I worked at the restaurant the more I learned about what was going on in this neighborhood. Supposedly all illegal activity ended when the next general election carried the reform movement into power. At least that is what I read in the Oakland Tribune.

Many, many years after my Uncle's restaurant closed I would still see one of the officers who received the payoff that I witnessed, still in police uniform, still patrolling the streets of Chinatown. I so wanted to talk to him about the changes that the Chinatown area had undergone during his tenure there as a policeman. As I watched him cruise down Eighth Street, I shook my head and said to myself that it was probably better to let sleeping dogs lie. I'll leave it to a dispassionate historian to chronicle the Oakland that I knew in the late 1940's.

**The author, left, with older brother Alfred,
and Adriano (Uncle Eddie) Jucutan, 1946**

adobo, pickled meat or vegetable dish with condiments

pansit, noodles with sauteed vegetables and meat

pinakbet, vegetable with meat stew

Ilocano, a Philippine Language

A PICKLE FOR THE SUN

Bill Sorro

When I was a child around the age of seven or eight, I used to hustle the Sun Reporter newspaper up and down Fillmore Street every Saturday morning. The Sun was one of the first Black newspapers on the west coast beginning around 1936. It was also the only Black newspaper in San Francisco. At that time, Fillmore Street was the heart of the City's African American community. The year was shortly after World War II, around 1947 or '48.

I'd pick up my papers early Saturday morning at the Sun's editorial office, down the street from Onorato's Fish and Poultry store, up on the second floor of a building located at the corner of O'Farrell and Fillmore. One morning I had to step over a man passed out in the doorway of the Sun. I was so frightened and scared that I couldn't bear to look down at him; I just knew he had to be dead. When I came back down the stairs with my bundle of papers, I held my breath. Much to my surprise and relief he was gone! In those days it was highly unusual to see someone drunk and passed out in the street…even in the Fillmore.

With my papers under my arm I would proceed to work one side of the Fillmore from Sutter to Fulton and back up the other side. " Sun Reporter mister? Sun Reporter ma'am?" For a nickel, of which I'd get a penny, you could get the latest news about what was going on in the Black community in San Francisco. And in those years, the Fillmore was the center and heart of the community. Until I was a very young man, I always thought the Fillmore was Harlem. For me it was.

Fillmore Street was alive on Saturday mornings…Saturday nights too! Small shops selling everything from dry goods to dry fish. Detters German delicatessen with so many different kinds of sausages, cheese and foods that we never ate in my home. What delicious smells! By the cash register was the largest jar in the world, full of dill pickles as big as your arm for only a nickel. "Hey, kid. Swap a paper for a pickle?" said the man behind the counter. Can you imagine a little kid trying to sell you a newspaper with a bundle of papers under one arm and a pickle, big as your arm under the other? "Sun, mister? Sun, ma'am?"

Wonderfully delicious aromas of fresh dark russian rye, pumpernickel and other baked goods wafted from the Ukraine bakery on McAllister and Webster streets, the center of a small Jewish community in the Fillmore. Permeating the air throughout the neighborhood was the smell of barbecue. And the very best in those days was the Kansas City Hickory Pit on Fillmore, nestled between the Long Bar Saloon (the longest bar west of the Mississippi), and the New Fillmore theater.

From the early 1940's, through the war years and into the early 1950's, large migrations of African American people settled in San Francisco, Oakland and Richmond. These migrations were a direct result of World War Two, especially the needs in ship building and the 'war effort,' as it was called in those days. Black people, other minorities and women were able to get jobs in the shipyards. My dad worked at AAA shipyard in Oakland during the war.

Fillmore Street was alive and bustling. People had good paying jobs and money to spend. And they did, right in their own communities. Mothers, fathers and kids shopping on Fillmore Street, buying food and other necessities for the week. You would always see or bump into people you knew. "Hey, Mama! There goes Mrs. Robles." "Hi, Sis! How are you?" The Delpinas or Campos family.

The San Francisco Filipino American community was very small in those years. In the Fillmore we all knew each other. There was always an unspoken, intimate connection that we shared as Filipinos, though not in any kind of cliquish or chauvinist way. We were Filipino and proud of it… and yes, we were family, too. In those days there was not the race identity of "Filipino American." As a matter of fact, in my home the use of the word "American" was to denote white people!

I'd sell all my papers, making most of my money in tips, working the bars along Fillmore. I knew every bartender working the Saturday morning shift. As long as I did not hassle their customers about buying a paper, they would let me work the bar. Always, you would meet a former newspaper kid, as the story went, and he would not only buy a paper, but give you a good tip, too! Now that's real class, ain't it?

From one joint to the next, there was always music. The beautiful sounds of Black music. Jazz, gospel, blues, boogie and swing. Up and down the block, around the corner, day and night, night and day. Music, music. Always music. Leola Kings Blue Mirror, Denny's Barrel House, The Long Bar, Chicago Barber Shop #1 & 2, Reds Shoe Shine, Uptown Bowl, Kansas City Hickory Pit, Manor Plaza Hotel…. "Paper, mister? Paper, ma'am?"

By the early 1950's, the Fillmore was becoming the west coast center of Black performing and visual artists, poets, writers, dancers and musicians, giving rise to what became known then as the Fillmore Renaissance.

Bobo Wado Fado Sabado. Everybody Loves Saturday Night. Indeed, the Fillmore was alive on Saturday night! The most prominent African American artists in the United States were to be seen and heard at one of the many night clubs, supper clubs, dance halls, ballrooms, jazz joints and other smaller venues. Johnson's Texas Playhouse, New Orleans Super Club, Club Alabam, The Plantation Club, Leola Kings Blue Mirror, Manor Plaza Hotel, Jimbo's Bop City, Jackson's Nook, Primalon Ball Room, Jacks of Sutter St.

The American entertainment and night club scene was totally segregated in those days. Racism, with few exceptions, had relegated Black performing artists to venues that were generally Black owned, operated and located in the community. From New York City, Chicago, Houston, Kansas City, St. Louis, New Orleans, Los Angeles, San Francisco and other little jazz and juke joints throughout this country. These clubs and joints became nationally part of what became known as the "chitlin circuit" for Black musicians and other artists.

By the time I'd finish selling my papers and paid the man at the Sun Reporter, it would be early afternoon. My belly would be full of all the good food given to me throughout the day by the baker, butcher, bartender, barbecue man and, of course, that pickle, which by now was only half eaten and wrapped in soggy newspaper and bulging through one of my pockets.

Coming home from Fillmore Street, approaching my house, I remember hordes of kids and young people always sitting, talking, playing and just cutting up as young people do. Inside our house some of my brothers and their friends would be playing *Boogie Woogie* on an old upright piano and dancing, always dancing.

When the kids were through, or if Mama got tired and ran them off, she would sometimes sit down at the piano and play herself. I would try and make myself invisible so that I would not distract her from playing. This was always such a wonderful treat, to see and hear Mama, my Mama, in a completely different context, playing the piano.

Mama was a short woman. Her legs could barely reach the piano pedals. When she played, her whole body seemed to be a part of the music, stretching her legs, standing straight up to reach the piano pedals that gave an added dimension, quality and tone to her music. I never could quite believe that this little woman sitting at the piano making this

171

beautiful music was my Mama.

La Paloma, Spanish Eyes, Begin the Beguine, For All We Know, I'll be Seeing You.......Music, music. Always music.

"Hey, mister! Paper? Sun Reporter, mama?"

THE GIFT

Elizabeth Marie Mendoza Megino

My mother, Angeles Grecia Amoroso Mendoza Jucutan, was born on August 2, 1904, in the Philippine Islands. At age 19 she accompanied her maternal uncle, Frederic Grecia from Jaro, Iloilo, on a ship to Manila. There he bought two tickets at $77.50 each for the trip by the steamship President Pierce to San Francisco by way of Hong Kong, Shanghai, Yokohama, Kobe, and Honolulu. Buying the tickets was like paying for a ferry ride across San Francisco Bay because no passports or visas were required. The Philippines was bought from Spain by the United States and was an American territory, and Filipinos were considered American nationals, not aliens. She arrived on May 3, 1923, in San Francisco, and unlike the Chinese passengers who were required to go to Angel Island for strict immigration processing due to the Chinese Exclusion law of 1882, she and her uncle were able to depart the ship and go on their way. Her uncle had brought her here to continue her education, but arriving near the end of the semester, he succeeded in getting her a job at the printing company where he worked.

When Uncle Fred left Oakland to go to Chicago, she asked her landlady how she might get a job that would enable her to go to school, and was advised to place an advertisement in the newspaper. She was hired by a couple of elderly Irish spinsters, Marie and Elizabeth Rickard, as a school girl with duties of helping with the laundry, housecleaning and some cooking which she learned from Marie. She eventually considered Marie her second mother since her own had died when she was 5 years old and her stepmother had treated her like the fairy tale Cinderella.

After graduating from Oakland High School and taking a course on the Victor 10-key adding machine and another one from the American Institute of Banking, she was able to get a job in the county assessor's office. However, her co-workers complained about her race, and she was soon laid off. She obtained other jobs and earned a decent wage, but the spinsters thought she was spending too much on Sundays going to the movies and dinner with her friend Maura Victoria who was one of the few Filipinas in the area. The Rickard sisters talked Mom into giving them her wages and in return they gave her a weekly allowance.

Later on, Mom married Antonio Judan Mendoza, whom she had met in her Spanish class in high school. They had a lot of trouble in renting apartments. The Rickards would usually rent the places for them, but as soon as other tenants found out they were Filipino, the tenants would force the landlord to evict them. It was even worse as the years went by and they had two children, my oldest brother and me.

At the time Dad had a job as a busboy at the Kress Five and Dime store on the corner of 14th Street and Broadway in Oakland. He was paid $17 a week without extra pay for overtime, and many times he would have to work ten to twelve hours a day. But in those days at least it was a job, especially since this was during the Great Depression.

In 1932, they were renting a house next to the gas station on the corner of Moss Avenue (currently MacArthur Boulevard) and Webster Street. During the week, when the spinsters would shop at the commission house, they would buy more fruits and vegetables than they needed, so they could give Mom a portion when they visited her on Sundays. They usually took my brother and me for a walk around the neighborhood or took us to Mosswood Park across the street from the gas station. This would give Mom a chance to do her shopping.

One day while on the walk, they saw this house for sale. It didn't have a lot of stairs which Mom preferred, and it had a large fenced backyard. Later on we discovered there had originally been a horse stable on the property.

Filipinos and other Asians were not allowed to buy land in California. When Mom, before she was married, gave her earnings to the Rickards and received a weekly allowance, she thought they spent the money on groceries and utilities because it was hard times for the two women also. But she found out they had saved every penny of it. She later wondered how they had survived during the Depression, and discovered they had sold many of the antique furnishings from their house. Elizabeth, while she worked, was also an antique collector, and after she retired she continued to go to antique shops. We have to remember that this was before social security and pensions. In order to have money after you retired, you had to either have saved while you worked, or you had to have invested the money in some income producing venture, usually stocks or real estate.

The Rickards presented Mom with the property as a "gift." They had bought the property in Elizabeth's name, placed the down payment using Mom's money, and turned around and transferred the title to her name. My mother had only to pay the mortgage and the taxes. They warned her to keep the property in her name, because Filipino men had the reputation of being notorious gamblers. They were worried Mom might lose the property if Dad or his relatives got hold of it. The usual custom among Filipinos at the time was when you had a room or apartment, you invited others to share it with you if they needed a place to live. Mom went against this custom and wouldn't let any of Dad's relatives move in while he was alive (he died in 1937). Mom lived in the same house for over 65 years.

During the 1930's, a petition was passed around in the neighborhood to evict our family, but Mom had been very diligent in paying her mortgage and taxes on time. Also one of the neighbors said that even though Mom was a widow and a single parent of five children, there wasn't a lot of noise from the house. We were always neat and clean, and Mom had the whitest wash in the neighborhood! When Mom found out about the petition she became very wary of her neighbors and she didn't tell her children about the attempted eviction until over 50 years had passed.

Mom, a courageous woman who stood up for her rights with dignity, now 97 years of age, is in a nursing home, cared for and nurtured by her loving family.

KISS THE GROUND

Tony Robles

Talkin' 'bout back home
>   like we've been there

Pictures
>   painted with closed eyes

Felt with hands
>   tracing the faces
Of the manong and manang

Tales from their voices
sung in the wind
Tasted in Kearney Street cafes

The creaky chairs
>   firmly planted and then
moved out
displaced
>   in a haste

But their stories are still heard

Ya know
>   my dad taught me to eat crab
>   the Pilipino way
Crack the shell
Take the yellow part

> the shit

And mix it with the rice

> Scoop it up with your hands

I closed my eyes

It was the first time I'd ever seen
The sun rise

And at that point
I understood my Lolo

> and the American dream

sweating under fedoras for pennies
in canneries a world away

> and what home really meant to him

And my Lola
And her children, my aunts, and uncles

Our roots
in ghettos firmly planted
and rising still

> Like Maya Angelou says

I

Painting the sky with our own dreams

But still
home calls us

We talk about it
like we've been there

Because
we have

SEVEN CARD STUD WITH SEVEN MANANGS WILD

Evangeline Canonizado Buell

Each week, Grandma invited Manang James, Manang Jones, Manang Brown, Manang Hawkins, Manang McQuinney and Manang Baldemero over for a serious game of high stakes poker. They were Filipino women elders, aged 40 to 60 at the time. Thus, I addressed them as "manang," out of respect and endearment. Most of the women, including my grandmother, were Filipino widows of African American soldiers who were stationed in the Philippines during the Philippine-American War. Unique in their West Oakland neighborhood, they were among the very few Filipino women living in the San Francisco Bay Area before WWII. No others shared their language and customs. For the most part, their existence was isolated and lonely. So these weekly card games at Grandma's were their prime social outlet.

Manang Rosario's hair cascaded all the way to her knees. Others had their black, waist-length hair pulled back and rolled into a bun at the back of their heads, fastened with Spanish gold combs and coil-shaped pins. Two of the younger women wore the trendy, short, permanent-waved hairdos of the day. They were the typical-size Pinays, five feet to five feet four inches, slim and delicate-looking, their skins the color of creamy ivory. The faces of the two older women were etched with well-earned lines of life. Their black eyes danced with excitement when they readied themselves for the game.

Grandma began preparing for the game early in the morning. As she cooked, the enticing aroma of sautéed onions and garlic engulfed the house. Then, soaked bean threads, shrimp and chicken would be added to the pot, and a scrumptious sotanghon noodle dish blossomed.

I was Grandma's ten year old helper then. I set up the poker table and chairs and tidied up the house. The women brought *biko* and *bibingka*, rice cakes baked in coconut milk and brown sugar. They steamed hot out of the oven, the aroma rich and tantalizing. I could hardly wait to eat. They washed down the delectable treats with Rainier Ale and ate with great gusto to the clinking sound of coins as they antied up.

The manangs sat around a green, felt-top poker table, opened their old worn purses and extracted both crumpled and crispy fresh bills. Digging down, they pulled out cloth bags bulging with coins won in past games. They piled the money carefully and methodically up front while

Grandma shuffled the cards. All the while they chattered incessantly in several dialects: Pampango, Tagalog, Ilocano, Visayan and broken English. "Hesusmariosep!," they swore colorfully, interspersing this expression with other savory expletives in various dialects throughout the game. At the end of each hand, the winner would squeal happily, "Oy, my goodness!" and scoop up the winnings.

They caught up on all the news about their families in the Philippines and their children and learned how to "cook American." Grandma complained, "I can't find lumpia wrappers," so she described how she created her own very thin eggroll pancakes and shared the recipe with the others. Canned tomato sauce was a good substitute for annato (achuete) seeds to add color to some of the special dishes. Making lemon pie was quite an accomplishment for Grandma. "Don't put too much cornstarch. And stir – no matter how tired you get," she said with pride.

When it came time to eat, I would hear all the different dialect-terms for rice – *kanon, nasi, enapoy, kanin* and *bigas*. "*Saing na*. Start cooking the rice." The manangs all had to learn Tagalog in order to communicate with one another here in America. One could understand why when there were five dialects for rice!

Manang Maria and Grandma Roberta both came from Pampanga and spoke its language with relish. Hungry for the sounds of their very own tongue, they savored and spoke each word reverently, like tones of gold. The others would rattle on in Tagalog, interrupting only to tell the two Pampanga manangs to quiet down or to translate once in a while, especially if it sounded like they were missing out on some juicy gossip. The manangs vibrated with charm, warmth and delight as they socialized and played cards. They were also tough and crafty gamblers.

During the game, they told stories about their lives, their struggle to live in America, their feelings of isolation, of being cut off from their families during World War II. They often felt unwanted in their new country and longed for the love and affection of their families so far away.

"*Mahirap dito sa Amerika.* Life is difficult in America," they said. But there was also acceptance, a resolve to persevere. "I might never go back to the Philippines. "

"I will die here."

"I stay with my husband."

"I must stay here to keep flowers on his grave."

I savored their feisty good humor and love of life which ensured their survival.

After much eating, chattering and several "Oy, my goodnesses," out came packages of cigarettes and cigars. They lit up, and the room became a silent haze of malodorous smoke. The game became exciting as the betting got intense. The silence was a blessed relief from the noisy chatter. The stakes were high, $50 to $200 was the norm. Cigarettes and cigars were held secure between the manangs' lips, some to one side of the mouth, others in the center moving up and down as the manangs giggled, talked and made bets. "*Makita kita.* I'll see you and raise $20."

I watched, captivated by their smoking — backwards, with the lighted end inside their mouths. How did they do that, I thought. The ashes didn't drop in their mouths and their tongues didn't burn. As they talked and laughed, cigarettes moved around their lips to the tempo of the chatter, the money piled high in the center. Still, no burning tongues.

"*Alam mo si Macario,* you know Macario, he ran away with a young *dalaga,* lass." They laughed, pulling the cigars out of their mouths in time to drop the long ashes into ashtrays, concentrating on seven-card stud, three down and four up.

One day I heard the manangs talking about a family. "*Maraming anak si Anna.* Anna has so many children. *Ang asawa, si Joey, walang trabaho.* Her husband Joey lost his job." I learned later that the manangs helped Anna and Joey buy food and clothing and pay rent with their winnings. The manangs also sent money home to the Philippines regularly to support their families. Winning was not just for themselves, but for others, and they expected nothing in return.

Many Filipinos, like the manangs, shared their resources with the Filipino community. Their homes were open to the Filipino men (later called manongs), who traveled back and forth from California farms to Alaskan fisheries, and often barred from staying in hotels and motels and eating in many restaurants. Often, these farm workers gave Grandma crates of fresh vegetables and fruits, like asparagus and tomatoes from Stockton. She and I would divide and pack them up to share with the manangs. After the poker game, each had a bag full to take home and they would reciprocate by leaving a *balato,* a tip, for the manongs.

The manangs mothered us children. We greeted them with hugs and kisses. Sometimes they asked me and my sister, Rósita, and cousin Rosario to play the piano or violin or sing for them. They took great interest in our development and school accomplishments. When they checked our report cards, they "ooh'd" and "aah'd, " praising us highly to our delight and awarded us *balato,* pin money from their "Oy, my goodness" winning pile.

"Here, this is for your lunch at school. You should not go hungry."

Or, "Spend this on books." I ran as fast as I could to the nearest comic book store.

"You must learn all you can. Education is important." Grandma proudly told them, "*Masipag sila.* They are hardworking." The manangs smiled with pride and called us *magandang dalagas,* beautiful young women, and we beamed as Grandma looked on approvingly. Sometimes there would be a new dress or shoes bought with the winnings from the manangs, especially when Grandma lost heavily. It would have been impolite for us to refuse the money or gifts.

At times, to ease their guilt and perhaps to salve their Catholic conscience, they would say, "Now, Ebanghelina, we want you to be good girl — no smoking, no drinking and no gambling. Very bad habit. Don't be like us. You be good woman." Little did they know, I learned great poker strategy from them despite their preaching. (To this day it is my favorite game, and my own grandchildren Joshua, Quiana, and Brielle, and I look forward to our mountain retreats every year so we can play like the manangs of long ago. It's poker chips, good food, but no smoking backwards, of course.)

During one game of five-card draw, I marveled at a loving maneuver of hands. Manang Nening said, "I open with $5." Manang Oping raised $10. Manang Maria upped the bet another $20. After a long pause, Manang Agapita blurted out, *"Makita kita! "*and ambivalently she raised $30. Manang Oping kicked her under the table. They continued playing. Soon there was a huge mound of bills and coins in the pot. Standing behind them, I caught a glimpse of the cards. One was holding a full house, another two pairs and another a straight. Then, with craft and skill, they purposely folded one by one so that Manang Rosario was left with the "winning" hand, a pair of tens. They had known she didn't have enough money to pay the PG&E and to buy groceries for the rest of the month. Her "Oy, my goodness" was music to their ears.

As the years passed, one by one the manangs folded. There were four and then three left to place their bets. I heard the last "Oy, my goodness" of the angels as they swooped down and opened their arms to scoop up to heaven the last remaining manang — my grandmother, Roberta.

Sitting front row: the author, father Estanislao Canon-izado, sister Rosita. Back row: cousin Rosario Garcia, Manuel Unabia, and grandmother Roberta Unabia, 1947

WHAT HAPPENS WHEN A MANANG DIES?

Jeanette Gandionco Lazam

Dedicated to all the Pinays that came before me, all the Pinays that stand with me, and all those who come after me and my generation of strong-willed sistahs!

We all know what happens when a manong passes on. He gets talked about at home, at the barbershop, the corner store, at the neighborhood restaurant, at the local newsstand.

But what happens when a Manang dies?

We all know that his friends will reminisce about the good old days, will miss him when they come to Chinatown to play pai gaw or at the horse races; sing sad and old songs of long ago; tip their hats in reverence and slowly move through life as though they will be the next in line to go.

But what happens when a Manang dies?

We all know that a manong is an icon, the true Filipino trailblazer - pioneer of sorts. As such, there is no more dancing or humming, laughing or joking, tickling and scratching, no more of anything.

But what happens when a Manang dies?

We all know that the end has come to the smell of stale cigars, heavy-starched white long-sleeved shirts, cuff links and tie clips, gray overcoats and shined shoes, pomade and greasy combs in the bathroom, and folded boxer shorts and Italian cut undershirts.

But what happens when a Manang dies?

We all know that our men folk want to cry but they don't. And we all know that we will never smell that Old Spice aftershave lotion, or hear the clink of the gold plated key chain as it swings in motion to unlock

191

the front door. We all know that a period of life, a slice of time will now be looked upon in photo albums and Sony camcorder videos of Lolo kissing the grandchildren and tickling them until they lose their breath.

But what happens when a Manang dies?

We all know that the tiyo's and tiya's will burn-up the telephone lines making arrangements for the last dinner, the last farewell to this Filipino old timer who braved the discrimination and prejudice of whites and others as he searched for employment and housing in the United States.

But what happens when a Manang dies?

We all know that come time to clean out his closet and dresser drawers, his wife, children and quite possibly grandchildren, will find things they never knew about him: girly magazines, nude women playing cards, unused condoms, Las Vegas and Reno one dollar coins, pictures of Jesus Christ and the Virgin Mary, bank books dated 1937 and earlier, an extra set of false teeth, his union cards, money clip, wrinkled and torn photos of him and his barkada in their army uniforms, cook and waiter outfits, and a 1941 snapshot of them standing on the footbridge in Central Park, dressed to the nines.

But what happens when a Manang dies?

Please tell me, what happens when a manang dies? We simply know because it rains softly and ever so gently, and then, we tuck her memory away deep in our heart and soul - for the loss is too great to deal with at the moment, and for an eternity.

Lolo, grandfather, adaptation of Spanish abuelo
tiyo, tiya, uncle, aunt, adaptation of Spanish tio, tia
barkada, very close friends, homies

THE TURNING POINT

Abraham F. Ignacio, Jr.

Like other communities of color during the 1960's and 1970's, the Filipino American community became involved with the struggles for civil rights and later to end U.S. intervention in Vietnam. The second-generation college age Filipino Americans on the west coast spearheaded the community's entry into broader political struggles of the time. Many of us joined the anti-war marches and student strikes for ethnic studies on college campuses. We began to question the second class status of Filipinos in American society. Many of us joined community struggles around issues like low-cost housing, equal job opportunity, immigrant rights and affirmative action. Out of these struggles arose a Filipino Identity movement among Filipino teenagers and young adults.

I reached a turning point in my life in the mid-1970's with the reading of a book – *America is in the Heart* by Carlos Bulosan. It was my first year in college at the University of California at San Diego. I was so captivated by the book I read it in one sitting. I could not put it down. The story it told of our people's experiences during the 1920's and 1930's brought out many different emotions and thoughts within me. At times anger seethed within me, then deep sadness took over. It was a book that was read by hundreds of my generation and revealed to us a history which was untold in our school books. It started me on a path to political activism in the Filipino community.

MY MANONG DAD, WAR BRIDE MOMMA, AND MAVERICK ME

Teresita Cataag Bautista

I was born in a kitchen on August 12, 1946, in Aringay, La Union, my father's hometown. After a month-long ocean journey in March 1947, my 20-year old mother, Florentina Catayoc Cataag Bautista from Ormoc, Leyte, and I docked in Seattle, Washington. Together with hundreds of World War II war brides and their babies, we arrived on the military tanker David S. Schenk. You can still see the military tanker dry-docked with the mothball fleet in the bay outside of Martinez, about 25 miles from San Francisco.

We took a train to re-unite with my father, Eutiquio Guillermo

Bautista, who was living in Oakland Chinatown after the war. He had returned to the States earlier with the U.S. Army First Filipino Infantry.

My dad had come in 1929, a youthful 19-year old. He worked the plantations in Hawaii and the seasonal farm work circuit up and down the west coast to Alaska. Mostly, he worked in hotels and restaurants. His co-workers named him Tex. I guess Eutiquio was hard to pronounce. Before the war, he worked at the Claremont Hotel in Berkeley, at the Yerba Buena Club on Treasure Island, and other restaurants in Oakland. My favorite place was the Robin Hood Inn, today a Vietnamese restaurant. He was still working for the Oakland Lucky's restaurant when he had his stroke in 1978, spent seven years in a wheelchair at home until he passed on during the holidays at the end of 1984.

My mom also worked hard in the fields, in the canneries, and in housekeeping. She became a self-taught dental technician and dental lab owner from the late 1950's to the mid-1980's. Now in her 70's, she works as a security checkpoint guard at the Oakland International Airport.

I am the oldest of four children. We all went to St. Anthony's Catholic School in East Oakland, where our classes had 50 students each. Our family's social life was filled with gatherings at homes of relatives and townmates that came over with my dad in the 1920's. They were our "uncles and aunties" who also left the Philippines to live in America. Some of them married in the 1940's during and after World War II. I remember mixed couples and their kids, Filipino Black, Filipino Mexican, Filipino Portuguese, Filipino Anglo, many of them living outside of California.

My mother was determined to send my two sisters, my brother, and me to Catholic school. We all had twelve years of Catholic education. At school, I felt comfortable about my ethnic identity since there were other Filipinos at St. Anthony's. It seemed that most of my classmates were children of immigrants then. Our school emphasized the diversity of the parish by sponsoring annual international festivals. Our physical education program highlighted folk dancing from around the world and we showed off our foot-tapping talents to the school-community in a school-wide event every spring.

For Filipinos, life during the 1950's seemed stable. Filipino communities grew slowly, since only fifty Filipinos were allowed to enter the U.S. each year since the 1934 Tydings-McDuffie Act. We were a community with low visibility. I can remember people always intrigued with what I was. I got used to, often irritated by, being asked, "What are you?" or "What nationality are you?" In fifth grade, we were studying current events and as the U.S. had its attention on a dictator Batista in Cuba, classmates were curious if I was related to Batista. "No, I'm not Cuban, I'm Filipino!"

For a while, I would make people guess my nationality, like a game that was okay when I was a teenager. After people would guess many things from Mexican, Japanese-Hawaiian, and even Alaskan Eskimo, I would exclaim over and again, "I'M FILIPINO!" There was the time during the summer of 1959 when my friend who lived on the corner and the rest of us girls were bored and fooled around on the telephone calling random numbers. Well, one of the boys we found at home wanted to come by and meet us. He came by and his first comment to me was "You're so dark!" Surprised, I thought to myself, "And you're ugly!" He left disappointed that he had not met a blonde, blue-eyed girl, just some Filipino and Japanese girls.

My identity was well nurtured as a child and established as a youth, since my family was very active in Rizal Post 598. The veterans, the women's auxiliary, and the youth groups met two Saturdays a month in the Veteran's Memorial Building. We grew up going to meetings, planning and sponsoring dances, learning and performing folkdances, cooking Filipino dishes, holding charity drives, and participating in parades through drills teams and majorette reviews.

I went to Notre Dame High School in Alameda. There were five of us from St. Anthony's who entered in the fall of 1960 – a Filipino, a Chinese, a Mexican, a Black, and a Redhead. We instantly integrated the all white girls school! I graduated as the "Most Likely to Succeed" in 1964. In my last year of high school, one of my friends and classmates heard that I was still an alien and did not have my citizenship papers. She quipped, "We should deport you for graduation!" I retorted that that was impossible, since I was senior class president and captain of the varsity volleyball team.

After entering San Francisco State in September 1964, I found myself intimidated with being immersed in such a massive student body, having come from a school of 320 girls. I found refuge in making friends with another Filipina, as we were combing our hair in the women's restroom. Our near-simultaneous question "Are you Filipino?" made us best friends until we transferred out of SF State. She volunteered for Vista and landed in an Indian Reservation in New Mexico. I didn't do well in my grades, distracted with a boyfriend from the Visayan Islands. He would come to campus all the time, and we would ride the M and J lines to the SF Zoo and Playland at the Beach. We ended our romance over our contrary views on the Vietnam War, where he drove an ambulance for the dead and wounded in the field. Years later I met him again, but he was still struggling with the trauma of the war.

I left SF State and entered Oakland City College, which became Merritt College on Grove Street. The school was well known for the Black Panthers who attended. It was the site of many teach-ins in support of liberation struggles around the world, in defense of native people's lands in America, and demonstrations against the draft, against the Vietnam War.

In 1966, moving out into my own apartment was a desperate break from a very strict and dysfunctional family environment. I wanted to be independent! My Pinoy friends chided me for leaving my family's house without getting married. It was scandalous. "You're going to be like those *puti* girls! They're all just *putas*." I was annoyed by their narrow views and felt no remorse.

Lovechild culture was permeating everyone's psyche. I felt an affinity with native peoples. I shared an apartment with a Mexican-American and a Peruana on Alcatraz Avenue near the Oakland-Berkeley border. It was common to take long walks up Telegraph Avenue to UC campus, even on late, hot summer nights. There was no fear of anything, and people were generally very mellow. My portion of the rent was $30 a month. I juggled three part-time jobs and 10 to 16 units per semester so I could get the education my parents expected – an unspoken mandate from a mother who couldn't afford to study past the third grade, and a father who finished at sixth grade. A working student for almost eight years, I would eventually be the first in my family to get a college education.

From 1966 to 1970 there were very few Filipinos in my social circle. I was part of a crowd of foreign students from all over the globe. Another striking experience then was when my boyfriend transferred from Merritt College to Cal Poly in San Luis Obispo. Upon hearing that he had a Filipino girlfriend, his roommate asked, "Does she have a tail?" I remember getting flushed, and saying over the phone, "You tell him when I come to visit, I'll show him my tail!" Shocked and offended, I didn't know until later why such a question would be asked. It was in the 1970's when working at Oakland Public Schools, where I trained teachers in multiethnic history, culture, and current concerns, that questions about Filipinos and monkeys would come up time and again.

When I finally transferred to UC Berkeley in 1969, I was mainstreamed my first year as an English major, a member of the college choir, and as a setter on the UC Varsity Volleyball Team. Up to then, I had an assortment of jobs to get me through school. I worked as a student clerk for Merritt's Foreign Student Adviser. In the evenings and weekends I sold patterns at New York Fabric's by City Hall. Before going downtown in the evenings I played with kids as a Recreation Leader in after school programs. My highest paying job, $3.50 an hour, twice the minimum wage then, was a two-year stint as a casual mail carrier at the Temescal Post Office. I resigned when I couldn't accept carrying all the election junk mail for Nixon's presidential campaign. The UC Educational Opportunity Program (EOP), landed me a job as an art history slide binder in the Bancroft Library. I was one independent woman!

At UC, I reconnected with Filipinos in 1970. We were over 40 strong in the Pilipino American Alliance (PAA). The next year brought me another work-study job at the International Institute of the East Bay (IIEB), where as Project Aide my assignment was to organize new arrival workshops which developed into the Filipino Immigrant Services (FIS) project. By graduation in 1972, I had my BA in Humanities and Inter-disciplinary Studies, but was also deeply involved as an organizer in Oak-land Chinatown. I gave up a Minority Scholarship in Education, I took a job in the Asian American Studies Department as a Field Work Assis-tant and led the sections on community organizing.

Inspired by the struggle to save the International Hotel in San Fran-cisco, student efforts went to building a low-cost hotel in downtown Oakland. The program, Project Manong, operated out of a three-story hotel being renovated for occupancy on 16th Street. Scores of students and youth conducted outreach to isolated and displaced seniors, who were "regulars" at the local pool halls and cafes in the Chinatown neigh-borhoods targeted for redevelopment and high-rise buildings. This out-reach was highly successful. Youth and young adults had come to respect the Filipino elders, our Manongs, for their contributions to the agribusi-ness industry of California and Hawaii. The young people were growing in the consciousness of themselves as Filipinos in the U.S. This knowl-edge compelled them to seek change in the living conditions of these dear elders, peers of their own fathers and grandfathers.

Martial law was declared in the Philippines in 1972. For the first time I saw masses of Filipinos in the streets, where I used to walk with hun-dreds of thousands of anti-war protesters. Now the focus was on Marcos and his military rule. This issue was one of the most controversial and polarizing debates in the Filipino community, lasting 14 years. Those of us who dared to take a strong position against Marcos were blacklisted, redbaited and, often silenced in community events. So many of us younger Filipinos understood the need for involvement in issues shaped by U.S. national policy affecting our community. We developed and provided leadership for resistance and protest to military oppression in the Philippines.

At the same time, the community response to issues affecting Filipinos in the U.S. because of racism and a lack of a strong Filipino voice in mainstream society was equally, if not more, engaging and controversial. Activists of all ages created community-based organizations. These groups addressed social, political, and economic needs of workers. I will be forever proud of my participation, and those of long-time friends, in building community institutions, like Filipinos for Affirmative Action, and groups that brought these issues to the awareness of government, funding agencies, and the broader community. We challenged backward community leadership that was self-serving and more interested in photo-ops with government officials.

I landed my first, full-time job in 1973 when I became the Filipino Liaison in the Office Community Relations for Oakland Public Schools. My anti-martial stance would find me in my supervisor's office every so many months. He would say, "I'm getting those calls again." Pro-Marcos community people would call him to complain, and even asked that I be discharged from my position because I openly criticized the Manila government. That was also the year I asked to join the Union of

Democratic Filipinos (KDP).

Besides going to junior and senior high schools to extinguish flare-ups and ease inter-racial tensions, I was able to train teachers on reviewing textbooks for omissions and distortions in books that mentioned Filipinos and the Philippines. We, the Filipino Far West Task Force on Education, went to Sacramento many times to lobby the California Board of Education. The group prepared citations from textbooks that reflected inaccurate and insufficient information on the Philippines and Filipinos in US history. It was quite an education to see how publishers lobbied officials and invested time to testify that their texts were relevant.

The Filipino community was so dynamic that initiatives abounded. We even had a local, bilingual TV program Asians Now on KTVU. Every Saturday morning we would see history, culture, and current concerns of the diverse Asian communities. For the first time, we saw our stories portrayed by us on television.

Before leaving the school district, I earned elementary and secondary teaching credentials. Again at UC Berkeley, the Black, Asian, Chicano Urban Program (BACUP) focused on cultural diversity and relevant education for minority students. These licenses opened up other opportunities in the school district. The adjustment of new arrivals and immigrants became my focus. I began to teach Vocational English as a Second Language (VESL) to Filipinos and coordinated and taught in employment training programs for monolingual and bilingual new arrivals from Asia. Today, it is not surprising that I work at a county hospital ensuring access to healthcare services for immigrants, refugees, and people who speak little or no English.

In between all of these events and involvement, I also became a mom. My 18 and 23-year old daughters reflect a strong sense of their Filipino identity, shaped by the circumstances that brought their third generation Irish-German father, a 1960's draft dodger, and me together. Eventually, I would find myself struggling as a single parent. They grew up around their Filipino family and relatives. Both girls have worked in community programs where Filipino issues were the focus.

I am at a stage in life where I am connected to my ancestors and our homeland. Friends, young and old, who treasure those who came before, keep me centered. In difficult times, we know we stand on our ancestors' shoulders. We seek to strengthen our continuing legacy from across the Pacific, where I began my life's journey.

---

puti, white

puta, prostitute

• Tydings-McDuffie Act, also known as the Philippine Independence Act, limited Filipino immigration to the U.S. to 50 per year.

• Union of Democratic Filipinos (KDP), a leftist Filipino American organization of the 1970's and 1980's that led protests against the Marcos government

1973
Tony Robles

Significant year for Dad and me
        I just moved in with him part-time
And we're getting acquainted

I'm wetting the bed
        And he don't understand
How come I don't want to eat
        Sleep
        Or go to the bathroom
Except when I'm asleep

1973
My Lolo is sick
In fact he's dying
Cancer
        They say from eating
Too much chili

Papa was a rolling stone
        is on the radio these days
and when I'm in the car with Dad
        and it comes on
it's very spiritual
        just can't explain it

1973

Do the guys that are singing it know
My Lolo?

     Did they write it for him?

1973
My Lolo dies

     But the funeral is delayed 'cause the
     Funeral directors are on strike
And his body sits a couple of weeks - waiting

Who'd think that the funeral business
     Ever went on strike?

1973
Watched more Soul Train than Bandstand
     Getting' to know Dad more
He's teaching me a lot
Namely - keep throwing the left jab to
Keep your opponent off balance, keep moving
Laterally and when you see an opening,
nail the motherfucker with the right hand

     George Foreman
Is the champ
But Muhammad Ali
     Is my hero

The Temptations are the only group around
And they're like uncles
To me

Skippin' to 1993
Dad has since moved to Hawaii
Has been there
Ten, fifteen years

Has got a glow from all the sun
For the first time ever
This dad is fun

Went to Colma to visit Lolo
But goin' back to '73
That must have been a damn good year
For those striking funeral motherfuckers
'cause when dad and I went to visit Lolo
at Holy Cross, it seemed like everybody
in the cemetary died in 1973

      all I saw on every stone was 1973

Made me wonder why they'd delay burying my Lolo
When there was so damn much business

      Goin' around

But
That's probably just my imagination

Then Dad said something

He said "When your grandfather came here as an
Immigrant...."
I had never tripped on that before
"Immigrant"
and neither had he
'Cause we all come
from
someplace
and all go
someplace
too

MAMANG'S GIFTS

Raquel Jumawan Willey

There's an old Filipino saying: "You can't go forward unless you know how to look back." I think there's truth to that statement because everything that I am now is the result of the daily decisions of generations before me. When I was younger my parents filled countless dinner conversations with reminiscences of family stories, little instances that were captured in their minds. It's amazing how remembrances were invaluable in giving me perspective about myself and the clan in which I grew up.

I visited my parents' place today to pick up some money for school. Even though I moved out of their house in San Leandro two years ago, I still come by periodically to get support. These visits are not easy for me. My flight away from the nest was a turbulent one, and to this day, after many hours of therapy and support from my own chosen family, I still find it hard to see them without going through some emotional backlash later on. I've gained enough distance, however, to allow myself to see these excursions as short archaeological digs from my past. It's just a matter of asking the right questions and finding the right opportunities.

Well, today I lucked out with both. My mother happened to be home and I had the mindset of asking her some questions about her birth family. So after some awkward greetings my mother and I settled down to eat lunch. "*Hindi ako kumain kaninang umaga.* I didn't eat this morning," she said, spreading out rice, *adobong manok,* and *nilaga* on the table. Somehow the familiar ritual of serving food comforted me a little; at least we have established some sort of truce between us, and perhaps I could have a decent conversation with her. We ate until our bellies were full.

"I want to know more about Mamang," I said, referring to my grandmother. We settled ourselves in the sala, sitting on opposite sides of the room on two different sofas.

Mamang was the only grandparent that I ever knew. She lived with my family for a number of years until she died in 1985 from the effects of a stroke which left her bedridden for months. At the time, my Kuya committed suicide in Oakland and we had to be flown hastily to the States to prepare for his funeral. My grandmother died a month later, and by that time I was too confused and sad to care about her death, so I never felt like I mourned her properly. Now, many years after her death, I wanted to get to know the woman who, through her kindness, inspired me to have my own life.

My grandmother lived with us until she died at 76. I remember her dimly as this old, fat, kindly woman who spent time with me and soothed me in times of sadness with coconut oil backrubs and soft croons in Ilocano. I loved her deeply, much more than I loved my mother and father, who seemed more interested in going to work than paying attention to me. My mother noticed this one day and almost begged me not to love Mamang more than her. That statement began a division between my mother and me that lasts to this day.

As the years progressed, I saw Mamang slowly deteriorate in senility and constant pain, and I realize now that I was angry at her for becoming so weak, especially when I needed her so much. Her death seemed like an admission of surrender to life, and that perception gave me the strength to vow never to be that weak in my own.

"Mamang?" Mom blinked.

"Yes. What did she do before she became a cop? Did she work a lot before Papang died? What was life like for you then?"

Those questions unraveled a family story I never heard before. Mom told me that, as a young woman, Mamang was a schoolteacher and Papang was a constabulary in Manila. By the time they got married and had children, the Japanese invaded the Philippines and began looting and burning Manila. My grandmother joined the women's unit in the Manila police force and my grandfather joined in the underground movement and had to constantly move from house to house to sleep to save his own life.

"When I was very young—I think I was five or six," Mom said, "I remember Papang carrying wounded men and sick men to our house, and Mamang nursed them back to health. I hardly saw Papang because Mamang said that 'Oh, he's sleeping in Uncle so-and-so's house.' That happened almost every night. I remember Mamang putting khaki colored blankets on malaria stricken men—you know, those men who look pale and shake a lot. I'd say we didn't have much of a normal childhood, because we were starving and scared of being killed all the time.

"I remember fire surrounding us. Manila was being burned by the Japanese and they kept getting our food supply. They also decapitated children on the streets. Yes, they were cruel that way."

She was nodding off to sleep. I don't think she was disinterested about what she was saying. I think that she doesn't want to think about how hard it was for her to have to be in a war and not knowing if her parents were coming back to protect her. When I pointed this out to her, she almost fell into a deep sleep, obviously not wanting to hear. I felt sorry for her.

Mom roused herself to continue with her story. She said that when Mamang joined the force, she took an exam and got the highest score. Mamang was made captain of the women's unit, the first of its kind in the Philippines.

"She led raids on prostitution houses. One time she busted a ring and arrested a woman who happened to be the mayor's girlfriend. When the girlfriend complained to the mayor, he demanded Mamang set her loose. Mamang said that it's impossible, since the girlfriend's fingerprints were taken already and the arrest was official. The mayor was adamant but Mamang stuck to her decision. She was fired from the force and the mayor, in his fury, abolished the women's unit.

"By that time Papang died and she had to find a job to support her family. She approached the fraternity Papang was part of, the Brotherhood of Masons, and asked for help. As a rule, once you're part of the Brotherhood, the fraternity is obligated to help your wife or widow. They gave her a job in the Manila Land Registry and she stayed in that job until she retired."

Mom told me that Mamang had to support her five children and her parents. She was hardly around and Mom told me fondly that her Lola Matea took her in as her favorite. "One time when I was crying she took my hand and we both went to the local sari-sari store. She fished out a big five cent coin—coins were bigger in those days—and bought me a Coca-cola. We took turns drinking until I stopped crying, then she gave me the change and said, 'Go ahead, keep it. You can buy yourself a bag of peanuts later.'" I was touched by the love coming from her eyes.

"You can't go forward unless you know how to look back".

I think it's that story about Lola Matea, my great grandmother, that opened my eyes to the connections between my clan's previous generations and my own. As a child, I couldn't understand why my parents constantly worked and left my brothers and I to the care of maids and my grandmother. It's that legacy, the loneliness and desperate fear, that lives in my parents still. Poverty and war drove Mamang's generation to work and survive at all costs; that decision caused the neglect of my mother and father. Years later, my parents still act like they're at war, working almost desperately to keep famine and danger at bay. None of the wealth and status they achieved gave them comfort, nor did they allow themselves to question whether their neediness would affect their children in any way. That legacy killed my brother.

Hearing my mother's narrative made me realize that it was my grandmother's influence that allowed me to make different choices in my life. I got into martial arts as a teenager—a reflection of Mamang's martial arts skills and training in the police force. I'm with a man like my grandmother, a tender, kind, and principled man. I'm studying to be a psychologist and, like my grandmother, I'll be called to do heroic acts in the line of duty. Most importantly, I'm allowing myself to be my own woman, just as Mamang allowed me to be myself around her.

I left my mother's house afterwards feeling that I've settled an old score with my mother. I did love my grandmother more than her, and for the first time, I felt good about it.

---

adobong manok, marinated chicken with condiments

nilaga, boiled meat with vegetables

sala, living room

kuya, elder brother

lola, grandmother, from Spanish abuela

CONVERGENCE

Helen C. Toribio

Time is slower after lunch. The bulk of barbecued oysters, Louisiana sausages, mangoes, and rice weigh in our stomachs. Above, the bright sun had evaporated every cloud, leaving a seamless blue sky. We are rendered motionless by the midday heat and the lethargic effect of food. Dad and I remain seated around the picnic table as the others disappear into the forest of Tomales Bay park. Mom makes a bed for herself under a juniper tree and falls asleep. Dad picks through the small pile of oyster shells he left on the table, muttering to himself how big they were compared to those in the Philippines. He sets aside two half shells, study-

215

ing them like an archaeologist. "I'll take these with me and show the folks back home in the Philippines how big the oysters are here." He speaks as though I am not there. His eyelids get heavy. The dark brown face under the baseball cap show sagging cheeks and thin lips turned black brown from a lifetime of chewing tobacco.

"You want to rest and lie down, Dad?" I ask. He and Mom had logged thousands of miles to be here, from the Philippines to Hawaii to San Francisco, then San Diego, and retracing the same route on the way back - all in four weeks time. This picnic was supposed to have been a rest stop for the seventy year old travelers. But I was the one who needed the rest. Without looking at me, Dad shakes his head, his eyes still on the oyster shells in his hands. It was a silly question to ask. I had said it out of common courtesy, not thinking who I was saying it to. He never took naps after lunch. Jet lags never seemed to bother him, either. A soldier, even a retired one, kept his habits. He was eighteen when he entered military life, beginning with the Philippine Scouts during the Second World War. When he joined the American Army after the war he must have developed an internal twenty four hour clock which he could set by moving the hour hand anywhere on the dial, anywhere he was sent to around the world. And that put him in real time, in real places, like this park where we now sat.

He pulls out a short braid of tobacco from its plastic cover and takes a small bite. His face awakens from the bitter chew. He looks at the ground around our picnic table, parts of it bare dirt, others covered with unmowed grass. I follow his area inspection and decide against an afternoon nap. I didn't take after lunch naps either, and the dirt and grass around us made it less inviting to consider one.

"Let's get some exercise," he says. In his baritone voice, those words come to me like orders from the master sergeant that he was. We walk along a narrow path which lead to the white sandy beach. On our left the forest of fir and oak trees allow a few streams of sunlight to break through the green canopy. To our right a cliff overlooks the calm waters of Tomales Bay. As we walk, we fall into our traditional roles of father and child. He, the storyteller of family tales. Me, the listener and learner. I expect recycled stories I had heard since childhood. Instead, I come to realize he is telling a war story. "It was like this," he says quietly.

I did not understand what he meant at first until I noticed how closely he watched our path, examining the ground as we walked, turning his head slowly to our left and right and above. Where I saw a peaceful forest around us, Dad saw a war zone.

米 米 米

A long time ago, as a young Philippine Scout, Teodoro Sudario Toribio - Dorong to family and friends - had hidden in a forest. He had escaped the Death March from Bataan, faking a fall and dropping himself into a ravine. He had expected rifle shots and machine guns to follow him as his body, rolling at its own momentum, crashed into bushes and trees. None came. But he expected death at the bottom of the chasm. The silence of the forest greeted him when he reached the valley floor. The pain from open wounds covering his body told him he was still alive. He removed his khaki uniform and buried it to avoid recognition from anyone that he was a soldier.

He paved his own path heading south towards Manila, sleeping with his ears to the ground in the darkness, resting behind bushes in daylight. The forest became his protective home where he measured time by the number of days between encounters with another human being. He could have remained in the forest for the remainder of the war if he wanted. Offers came from people he met along the way. He helped an elderly farmer clear his land and plant his rice seedlings. The old man, having no hope that his own son would return from the war, bid the young soldier to live with him. Dorong said thank you, but he had to move on.

Then, along a river he met a young widow carrying a baby on one arm, a cloth bundle on the other, and another bundle balanced on her head. She backed away from him when he approached her to ask what area he was at. When she would not answer his question, he walked passed her. And she said, "Capoocan." He was not far from Manila. He asked her for directions to the nearest town. She was on her way to her parent's village near the town, she said. If he would help carry her bundles, they could reach the town in two days. He slept a distance from the woman and child that first night they traveled together. He did the same the second night only to find her warm body next to his during the coolest hours before daybreak. He got up, reminding himself where he had to go. "Please," she said, "My husband is dead and my parents are aged. I could not care for them and my baby alone."

He was tempted to touch the smooth face of the young woman and run his fingers through her long black hair that morning. But he quickly packed up her bundles and saw her to her village. He bid her good-bye before her parents saw them together.

In the outskirts of Manila he was warned by a fisherman not to return to the city just yet. The area was still surrounded by the enemy. The fisherman invited Dorong to live in the fishing village with him. He helped the fisherman gather oysters in the shallow waters of Manila Bay. For a few days the calm waters and the silent forest behind the village made him forget about the war.

He was brought back to the war when enemy soldiers paid a visit to the village. A Japanese officer had been killed. A Filipino guerrilla had been suspected and they were searching for him. The Japanese soldiers confronted Dorong and the fisherman where they stood gathering oysters in the water. One soldier came face to face with the Scout who was dressed like a fisherman. The soldier demanded to know if the young fisherman had seen any strangers in the village. Dorong remained silent. The soldier raised his voice higher and asked the same question. The Scout's face tightened. The soldier asked again, shouting this time. When no answer came, the soldier whipped his hand across Dorong's face.

The older fisherman put himself between the Dorong and the soldier, bowing intermittently. "Please, please. Forgive my, my son. He does not speak much. He is a very simple boy. He and me, we fish all day, everyday, so we don't know if strangers come by our village." With a smirk the enemy soldier stepped back and left the village with his companions.

That night a livid Scout demanded to know who had a gun in the village so he could kill the soldier who had slapped him. The older fisherman sat him down. "I can tell you where you can find a gun," said the fisherman, eyeing the young man with a hard look. "But think what would happen if you kill that Japanese soldier. You kill him and they will come here to kill everyone in the village."

Dorong left the village shortly after he was made to swallow his anger. In Manila he headed for MacArthur's headquarters where he got his orders to join a unit which needed a Scout who knew his way in the jungle.

✳   ✳   ✳

As my father told his story I, too, became more conscious of the forest. The sound of crushed twigs as we walked along the narrow path of moist dirt. Sunlight sprinkling through leaf covered branches above us. The rustle of leaves when birds took flight. I was revisiting a place in time with my father, witnessing the choices he had made. A war had offered him other possibilities. A farm life, a different wife, a revenge he could have fulfilled. He chose, instead, a different path, one which ultimately led to one we both walked on. Here, in this forest our lives converged. Two places ten thousand miles and fifty years apart were merged through a memory relived.

A SPECIAL STORY

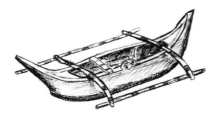

NEW COUNTRY

Mary Bonzo Suzuki

The first place we lived when we landed in the United States was the Eddy Hotel on Eddy Street in San Francisco. All five of us in one hotel room. Four children and one parent. All severely bloated with malnutrition. Skinny with swollen tummies. Kwashiorkor they called it. Our skinny bodies did not stop our exploring and inquiring spirits. Younger sister used the bathroom, she flushed the toilet and started screaming for help because of the noise. Next she found herself unable to get out for somehow she had double locked the door. The maintenance men came and tried to quiet her down so they could tell her how to let herself out. They did not succeed. They broke the door open. A swollen faced, snotty nose, frightened child fell out of the bathroom. Mother collected her in her arms. Sister sobbed louder.

We all crawled into the two beds early. Without any dinner. American food would not settle into our starved bodies. All the girls and Mama into the two beds. The hotel brought up a cot for brother. The room shook with our fitful sleep and our terrible dreams.

The next morning brother and I were up early. Dressed. Down stairs and out into the street. The street in front of the hotel was filled with men sprawled on their bellies, some curled up. Bodies so utterly still. We ran back to the room. We yelled that there had been a bombing and many were dead outside. Mother woke quickly and told us to be quiet. "Those are drunk men." "Drunk? What's that?" we asked in unison. Mother hushed us.

The same day, the social worker took us to a department store. She didn't think our khaki's, given to us by the U.S. military in the Philippines to cover our various stages of nakedness, were a good idea in San Francisco. We hadn't noticed. The two younger sisters balked at the step of the escalator. The moving stairway scared them. Mother led them to the elevator. Brother and I loved the 'moving stairs.' We met them in children's clothing. Two hours later, Mother and social worker lined us up and beamed their approval. We wore new clothes from neck to toe. All four of us were now dressed in every color of the spectrum. We felt stiff and self conscious.

Time to try eating again. This store had a cafeteria. We each took a tray and slid it down two silver tracks. There were food selections to be made every inch of the way to the cash register. Nothing looked familiar. I stopped at the cottage cheese.

I spat it out. It was icy cold and soft. "Disgusting," said my stomach as it spasmed. Mother groaned. She despaired of ever feeding us again. The social worker helped me clean up. She rounded us up and marched us to the door of the store. In no time, we were in Chinatown.

She seemed to know the place. "Hi, Charley," she greeted the man at the cash register.

Seated at the table, we were served real food! First the soup of seaweed and tofu. Then some fish, rice, and vegetables, including eggplant and bitter melon. All of us kids grinned, laughed, and said, "thank you" in unison. Our eyes and minds knew these foods. Our body cells communicated, "Eat!" Our digestive apparatus accepted the food. Mother and the social worker talked with our Chinese-Filipino host. We children solemnly ate. Charley understood we were from the Philippines, his old country. He gave us more food - on the house. "Come to eat anytime, all the time," he urged, "breakfast, lunch and dinner, come!" His face beamed.

We stayed at the Eddy hotel for a month. We ate everyday at Uncle Charley's restaurant. Mother found a job at the library. She was not as lucky in finding housing. She decided to move to Lincoln, Nebraska, where she had gone to school. This began our new life in the United States of America.

MAMA'S CLEANERS

Marie Mendoza Rivera-Yip

It was the year 1942, Pearl Harbor had been bombed, Japan and the U.S. were at war.

Our family's Japanese friends and neighbors, U.S. citizens, were being rounded up and shipped to internment camps. My mother, Maria Mendoza Rivera decided to buy a cleaning and laundry establishment from her Japanese family friend. Mom didn't have the $385 to purchase the business so she borrowed the money from a willing cousin.

Before mom's friends left for camp, they invited our family to have dinner with them. They needed to negotiate the terms of the sale before they departed. I remember being afraid to eat, because all I had heard on the radio was how the Japanese were killing people. I was eight years old

225

at the time, and just before I sat down at the table, I cried out "Mama! Mama! They're going to poison my food! They're going to kill me! I don't want to eat. Please don't make me eat their food!"

"You come with me right now, Marie." She took me aside gave me a spanking, and said, "You get back in there and eat your dinner."

Mama's Cleaners was in the heart of Oakland Chinatown at 816 Franklin St.. The storefront had blue and white tile halfway up and glass to the ceiling. As one entered the Cleaners there was a counter where the packaged laundry was stored. The pressing machine loomed up behind the counter. The pressed clothes were hung on racks along the walls. Past the racks were two single beds which were hidden behind a hanging sheet. There was a dark hall leading to the bedroom and kitchen, and at the end of the hallway an enclosed toilet.

My mother ran the Cleaners alone. My dad, Stanley, worked at a restaurant a few miles away. The actual cleaning and laundry were done by other companies. The garments were picked up and returned for mom to do the pressing. I'd watch her iron as she smoked with the lighted end of the cigarette in her mouth. The steam of the pressing machine mingled with the smoky haze. Many of the Filipina women of her generation smoked backwards. The Cleaners became a meeting place for a lot of Filipinos. Most nights there were people at the dinner table. Many of them were the manongs who hung out at the pool hall down the block. They were lonely for family and a home cooked meal. Mama was their substitute mother.

At the corner of 8th and Franklin streets was a gas station, and Wong's Restaurant where we ate many meals. I'm still friends with the owners daughter, Jen Wong, after 60 years. In the middle of the block was Dr. Yee's office our family doctor, then Mama's Cleaners, and a noodle factory where mom bought pancit noodles. Walking along to 9th street was a newsstand/candy store where I spent my pennies on tootsie rolls, then on to the barber shop where my brother Stanley got his monthly haircuts.

My parents lived in the quarters behind the Cleaners, and I lived with my married sister Lenora because I was scared of the cockroaches. The Cleaners was dark and smelly and when you turned on the lights at night the walls were covered with thousands of cockroaches that scampered into the woodwork of the old building.

My Mama died in 1947 when I was 12 years old. The Cleaners closed, ending a chapter of my life.

Marie Mendoza Rivera-Yip

BIOGRAPHIES

The Writers

Joseph T. Oliva Arriola is a motivational speaker, lawyer, and practitioner of Kamatuuran (truth) philosophy. In another life, he grew up in a pool hall, learned how to stickfight, and cut lettuce as a farmworker. He is married to Donnalynn Rubiano and is father to Felinn and Jehlia.

Gloria Balanon Bucol lives in Fremont, California, and is currently an assistant principal for New Haven Unified School District's (Union City) adult education program. She is the mother of three children: Steven, Nikki, and Scott Bucol. The greatest impact in her life has been the loss of her two beloved sons, Steven in 1980 and Scott in 1999.

Teresita Cataag Bautista is a 1.5 generation Pinay born in Aringay, La Union, and an early Baby-Boomer born after World War II She was raised in Oakland, California, and has been active in community services and advocacy for the past three decades. A founding member of Filipino Civil Rights Advocates, Filipinos for Affirmative Action, Katipunang ng mga Demokratikong Pilipino and California Healthcare Interpreters Association, her efforts continue to improve the quality of life of immigrants and new arrivals.

Evangeline Canonizado Buell was born in California, raised in the Bay Area, and lived all of her adult life in the city of Berkeley. Her professional goals have focused on promoting cultural understanding on both the local and international levels. She served as Public Events manager of International House at U.C. Berkeley and Program Coordinator of the Consumers Cooperative of Berkeley, Inc. She taught Folk Guitar for 25 years and has performed on concert stage, radio, and TV. She is the recipient of several awards for community activism and received the Filipino American National Historical Society Silver Arts and Music Award. She currently serves as president of FANHS East Bay Chapter. Vangie is married to Bill Buell and has three daughters, Danni, Nikki, and Stacey Vilas, two grand daughters Quiana, and Brielle, and one grandson Joshua. Vangie's parents were born in the P.I. and they came to the U.S. in the 1920's.

Trudy Bonzo Chastain was born in Cavite, Philippines in 1940. She and her family came to the U. S. in 1945. They lived in Nebraska two years before coming to Stockton, California in 1947. Trudy went to Scatter-good High School in Iowa and then to U.C. Berkeley. She lives in Richmond, California with her husband Charles. They have two sons, Michael of New York and John of Richmond.

Willie Fernandez is a first generation Filipino American living in the Bay Area, enjoying his grandchildren and using his social work, human resources and legal background to help people find the best way to get things done.

Eleanor M. Hipol-Luis is East Bay born and raised, was a kid in the 50's, survived the 60's and approached adulthood in the 70's. She is married to Ben Luis and they have three sons: Joachim Maximo, Paulo Tomas, and Valentino Augustin. "My family has taught me what grown up real-ly means, and we continue to grow together."

Abe Ignacio, Jr. is a second generation Filipino American born and raised in San Diego, California. He is a navy brat and spent four of his adolescent years in the Philippines. He hopes to be fluent in Pilipino by the time he turns fifty.

Herb Jamero is a second generation Filipino American has written stories and poems, mainly about his heritage, many of which have been featured in the Filipino Journal and other publications. He is a retired Psychiatric Social Worker specializing in youth and families. He now resides in Livingston, California on the family ranch—the original site of the Jamero Farm Labor Camp which housed up to 100 Filipino farm laborers during the peak harvest seasons. This background provides the impetus and inspiration for his stories and poems. He is the Historian of the Central Valley Chapter of the Filipino American National Historical Society—FAHNS—which is dedicated to the documentation of the Filipino American experience.

Peter M. Jamero was born in 1930 and raised on a farm and Filipino farm labor camp in Livingston, California, he is the eldest son of Filipino pioneers from Bohol. He went on to achieve numerous "Filipino American Firsts" in government while also serving on Filipino community organizations and boards. He has 30 years of top level executive experience in local, state and federal government; directed programs with budgets of up to $42 million and staff of more than 400; and was on the faculty of a teaching hospital of a major university

Brenda Manuel After losing my mother in 1996, I felt lost and as though part of my Mexican heritage was completely gone. For many, many years I felt the same way, losing my Filipino father at age 7. When I began writing with the East Bay FAHNS organization in Berkeley, I was flooded with vivid memories of my mother and father. Some were painful stories to write and others were easily written. My stories are the rich memories I have of growing up Filipino and Mexican. With these stories came a feeling of healing and a wholeness of who I am today.

Benjamin Mendoza was born in Oakland, California in 1934. Attended Oakland Technical High School and the University of California, Berkeley. My wife, Patricia, and I have three daughters and three grandchildren, two boys and a girl. I am retired from the Lawrence Livermore National Laboratory. This story is from my "Remembrances: A compendium of vignettes."

R. Baylan Megino-Cravagan Born and raised in the San Francisco Bay Area, I am the middle child of first and second generation parents. I am a bridge between generations, cultures, peoples, ways of being and varying shades of colors of light and movement. My life is a continuous journey of discovery and sharing the strength and texture of the deep roots that hold such a bridge in place.

Elizabeth Marie Mendoza Megino was born and currently resides in Oakland, California. The second of five children of Filipino pioneers Angeles (97 years old from Jaro, Iloilo) and Antonio (from Pagdalagan, La Union), she and her husband Honofre have three daughters: Stephanie (Los Angeles), Rosalinda (El Cerrito) and Catherine (Phoenix) and three grandchildren: Cristopher, Caroline and Steven. She retired from the University of California at Berkeley as the undergraduate adviser for the majors of Asian American Studies and Ethnic Studies.

Mel Orpilla is currently the director of Youth Strategies for the city of Vallejo's Fighting Back Partnership. He is the executive director of Filipino American Social Services. He is the founder and president of the FANHS Vallejo Chapter. He is a regular columnist for the Vallejo Times-Herald writing about the Filipino experience in America. As a volunteer, he sits on various boards and commissions in Vallejo. He attended Solano Community College, CSU Sacramento and San Francisco State University where he earned degrees in photojournalism and ethnic studies.

Loralei Cruz Osborn is second generation Filipino American. She lives in San Francisco with her husband Richard and daughter Alina. Projects include creating the website for the Filipino American Center at the San Francisco Main Library and compiling online resources for Filipinos in the United States: A Print and Digital Resource Guide. Currently she is a part-time student pursuing a degree in library and information science at San Jose State University and works as an information specialist.

Tony Robles is a native San Franciscan. Learned to write by listening to the laughter of his uncles. When he's not writing, he loves eating Chinese food, listening to old songs by the Temptations, and taking long naps.

Victoria J. Santos is a human resource professional specializing in workplace cultural diversity. She is one of "Workers' Dozen," a monthly feature in the San Francisco Chronicle dealing with work/career issues. She was the first director of Filipinos for Affirmative Action. She continues to enjoy foreign travel with her husband Nuno and son Thomas.

James Sobredo was born in Iloilo City and raised in Guam. James Sobredo came to the United States when he was four and grew up speaking Ilongo, English, Tagalog and Chamorro. He has a Ph.D. in Ethnic Studies from U.C-Berkeley and is currently an assistant professor in Asian American Studies at Sacramento State University. He and his wife Lourdes are life-time members of FAHNS and have a six-year-old son named Adrian.

Bill Sorro is a native San Franciscan, second generation Filipino American, father of six children and ten grandchildren, former International Hotel tenant and activist to save the I-Hotel, and active in labor and community work and struggle for social and economic justice for over thirty years. He is currently active in the Mint Mall Organizing Committee of the South of Market Filipino Community in its fight against gentrification and displacement. Also currently a board member of the new International Hotel Senior Housing Project/Manilatown Heritage Foundation and United Pilipinos Organizing Network. "My belief is still that revolutionary change and economic transformation in favor of the masses of American people and our working class is essential if we are ever to achieve equality, justice and to eradicate poverty as we know it today."

Mary Bonzo Suzuki was born in Chicago, Illinois. Her parents met at the University of Nebraska. They had to go back to the Philippines due to the violence they faced here and no employment. She spent her childhood and early adolescent years in the Philippines. After WWII they were repatriated – those of the families that survived the war. She came to Berkeley to study at U.C. and worked her way through and completed her doctorate. She married an artist, Lewis Suzuki. They have two children and three grandchildren. They are all used to her scribbling. Their eldest granddaughter also writes stories and another granddaughter paints. Her grandson builds intricate structures. She taught for over thirty years.

Helen Caubalejo Toribio was born in Leyte, Philippines, and grew up in Hawaii. A cultural and civil rights activist, and supporter of human rights in the Philippines, she currently teaches Asian American Studies at City College of San Francisco and at San Francisco State University.

Raquel Jumawan Willey was born in Quezon City, Philippines on April 11, 1971. She came to the U.S. in March, 1985 after her older brother Joel died. Currently she is a Ph.D. student in psychology at the California School of Professional Psychology.

Marie Mendoza Rivera -Yip was born in Oakland California, raised in the Bay Area and lived all her adult life in and around the Bay Area. Twenty seven years in the Montclair area and the last seventeen years in Hayward. Attended Oakland High School and Merritt Junior College. Worked for the Federal Government, retired from Alameda County as a Patient Services Technician. Marie is a widow, has three sons, Michael, Ronald and Brett, and three daughters, Rhonda, Kimberly, and Christine, 2 grandsons Daniel and Myasha, 3 grand daughters Kristina, Candice and Elenita. Marie's parents were born in the P.I and they came to the U.S. in the 1920's.

The Artists

Carl Angel was born in Bainbridge, Maryland and grew up in Honolulu, Hawaii. He received his Bachelor of Fine Arts from the Academy of Art College in San Francisco. He is a painter and illustrator whose work is exhibited in galleries and museums throughout the Bay Area. Angel is also the illustrator of numerous children's books, including *Mga Kuwentong Bayan* and *Willie Wins,* and his artwork is included in the children's anthology *Honoring Our Ancestors.* He lives in Oakland, California.

Lewis Suzuki was born in Los Angeles and currently lives in Berkeley, California. He studied art in Japan, Los Angeles, New York, and Oakland, California, and is "known for his bold impressionistic use of color... and has integrated western watercolor techniques with Japanese calligraphy to produce a strong, well-defined style."

"For Mr. Suzuki, art is an important and integral part of life and should, therefore, enrich and strengthen the human spirit. Through his art he would like to give people a sense of joy and hope in our difficult and changing world."

He is the recipient of "numerous Best of Show, First Prize, Purchase Awards, and other awards from various regional and national shows."

A FILIPINO AMERICAN TIMELINE

1587

The Spanish galleon La Nuestra Señora de Esperanza drops anchor at Morro Bay, California. Its crew includes a small number of "Luzones indios," the first recorded arrival of Filipinos to the Americas.

1788

The British ship Iphigenia Nubiana is reported to arrive in Cook Inlet, Alaska, with a crew that included a "Manilla man."

1870

The Sociedad de Beneficencia de los Hispano Filipinos de Nueva Orleans (Benevolent Society of Hispanic Filipinos of New Orleans) is founded, suggesting a hispanicized Filipino American community had been established in the U.S. since at least the 1860's.

1898

Under the pretense of helping the Filipinos gain independence from Spain, Admiral George Dewey enters Manila Bay in May. After an inconsequential fight, Dewey and the Spaniards act out a mock battle of Manila Bay as a way for Spain to "honorably" surrender to another western imperial power, rather than admit defeat to the Filipino revolutionaries who had effectively liberated most of the Philippines from Spanish colonial rule. In December, the United States negotiate the Treaty of Paris, transferring to the U.S. the control of former Spanish territories: Guam, Puerto Rico, Cuba, and the Philippines. For $20 million, the U.S. "buys" the Philippines from Spain (without the knowledge nor consent of the

Filipino people). Meanwhile, preparations were underway to militarily secure the Philippines for U.S. occupation. Senate arguments for and against ratification of the Treaty of Paris and the high-priced acquisition of the Philippines generate intense national debate in the U.S. The growing presence of the U.S. military in the Philippines likewise intensifies the political dynamics in the Philippines.

1899

On February 4, shots exchanged between American and Filipino troops spark the beginning of the Philippine American War. Two days later, the Treaty of Paris is ratified by the U.S. Senate. Over 100,000 U.S. troops are sent to the Philippines, volunteers from nearly every state embark across the Pacific Ocean from the Presidio in San Francisco.

1900

U.S. census Filipino population: no count, although U.S. presence of Filipinos were known. Even though the Philippines was already U.S. territory, census of the island population was separate from the U.S. census.

1902

The Philippine American War, commonly called the "Philippine Insurgency" in American history books, is declared ended by President Theodore Roosevelt. President Roosevelt later officially opens Union Square in San Francisco to honor America's supremacy over the Philippines, and features a tower memorializing Admiral Dewey's "victory" in Manila.

1903

The pensionado program sends selected students from the Philippines to U.S. colleges.

1904

The St. Louis World Exposition highlight the $1 million Philippine "reservation" featuring 1200 Filipinos from various tribes of the Philippines, pensionados as tour guides, and Philippine Scouts as guards.

1906

Arrival of first Filipino sakadas (sugar cane workers) to Hawaii

1910

U.S. census Filipino population: 2,767

1919

Hawaii Sugar Planters Association establish offices in Philippines to begin full scale recruitment of Filipino contract laborers for Hawaii sugar cane plantations.

The Filipino Federation of Labor founded by Pablo Manlapit.

1920

U.S. census Filipino population: 26,634 (863% growth from prior decade)

1920 – 1934

Mass migration of Filipino laborers to Hawaii and west coast. Anti-Filipino race riots throughout California, e.g. Stockton, Exeter, Watsonville

1921

Philippine Independent News founded in Salinas, California

1924

Striking Filipino sugar cane workers clash with police resulting in the Hanapepe Massacre on the island of Kauai, Hawaii.

1929

California state legislature calls for federal immigration restriction of Filipino labor.

1930

U.S. census Filipino population: 108,424 (307% growth from prior decade)

The Filipino Federation of America clubhouse in Stockton is bombed.

Fermin Tobera, a laborer, is murdered in Watsonville generating a National Day of Humiliation in Manila with a mass demonstration of 10,000.

1933

Salvador Roldan vs. Los Angeles County challenges the anti-miscegenation law of California which bars marriage between whites and non-whites.

State of California add the term "Malay" to its anti-miscegenation law to prohibit Filipinos from marrying whites.

1934

The Tydings-McDuffie Act promises Philippine independence and restricts Filipino immigration to the U.S. to 50 per year.

1935

Congress passes the Filipino Repatriation Act to provide a one-way passage to the Philippines and prohibit return to the U.S.

1940

U.S. census Filipino population: 98,535 (9% decrease from prior decade due to Great Depression and effects of the Tydings-McDuffie Act).

1941

After the bombing of Manila and Pearl Harbor by Japan the U.S. goes into war, and opens recruitment of soldiers from all ethnic/racial groups.

1942

The all Filipino First and Second Regiments are established, and U.S.-based Filipino soldiers are granted U.S. citizenship.

1943

Publication of Carlos Bulosan's *America is in the Heart*.

1945

Congress passes the War Brides Act allowing the wives and families of U.S. servicemen to immigrate.

1946

Congress passes two Rescission Acts denying benefits to Filipino veterans of WWII who fought under U.S. command in the Philippines.
U.S. "grants" independence to the Philippines.

1948

Vicky Manalo Draves wins two Olympic gold medals for diving, becoming the first American woman to win more than one gold in an Olympic game.

1950

U.S. census Filipino population: 122,707 (25% growth from prior decade)

1952

Pioneering Filipino American labor leaders Chris Mensalves and Ernesto Mangaoang face red-baiting charges, placed under deportation proceedings, but subsequently acquitted.

1960

U.S. census Filipino population: 176,310 (44% growth from prior decade)

1961

Founding of the Philippine News in San Francisco.

1965

The Immigration and Naturalization Act liberalize immigration to the U.S.

Filipino farmworkers in Delano initiate the grape strike that leads to the formation of the United Farmworkers Union.

1967

United States Supreme Court rule anti-miscegenation laws as unconstitutional.

1968

Elderly manongs begin efforts to save the International Hotel in San Francisco.

College students whose leaders included Filipino Americans at San Francisco State University walk out on a Third World Strike that eventually lead to the creation of ethnic studies.

1970

U.S. census Filipino population: 343,060 (95% growth from prior decade).

Activism and population growth due to immigration highlight community development throughout the decade. With a critical mass Filipinos in urban areas, community activists begin to address issues of immigrant rights, bilingual education, low income housing, and senior citizens, and the licensure of Philippine-trained professionals such as nurses, dentists, and medical technologists.

1970-75

Formation of numerous community and college based programs in cities across the U.S. to serve Filipino Americans, e.g. Filipinos for Affirmative Action in Oakland, and Pilipino American Collegiate Endeavor (PACE) at San Francisco State University.

1971

The First Filipino People's Far West Convention is initiated by community activists in Seattle and held annually in different west coast cities until 1981.

1972-75

Formation of several U.S.-based organizations opposed to martial law in the Philippines, e.g. the National Committee for the Restoration of Civil Liberties in the Philippines (NCRCLP), Katipunan ng mga Demokratikong Pilipino (KDP), Movement for Free Philippines (MFP), and the Friends of the Filipino People (FFP).

1977

Filipino Americans organize a national campaign to defend immigrant nurses, Filipina Narciso and Leonor Perez, wrongfully accused of murders at the Veterans Hospital in Ann Arbor, Michigan.

1980

U.S. census Filipino population: 774,652 (126% growth from prior decade)

1981

Assassination of labor, community, and anti-martial law activists, Gene Viernes and Silme Domingo in Seattle, and the creation of the Committee for Justice for Domingo and Viernes which successfully win a wrongful deaths civil suit against Ferdinand and Imelda Marcos by the end of the decade.

1986

Filipino Task Force on AIDS is established in San Francisco. Filipinos are found to have highest AIDS cases among Asian Americans.
Founding of the Filipino American National Historical Society in Seattle.

1989

Filipinos are removed from the affirmative action list in the University of California system.

1990

U.S. census Filipino population: 1,422,711 (84% growth from prior decade)

Congress passes the Immigration and Naturalization Act which grants U.S. citizenship to Filipino veterans of WWII.

1991

East Bay Chapter of FANHS is founded.

Vallejo Chapter of FAHNS is founded.

1994

Filipino Civil Rights Advocates (FilCRA) is founded in Berkeley.

Benjamin Cayetano of Hawaii becomes the first Filipino American elected as state governor.

1999

Joseph Ileto is gunned down by a white supremacist in Southern California.

2000

U.S. census Filipino population: 1.8 million (31% growth from prior decade)

GLOSSARY

Adobo: marinated or pickled pork, chicken served hot

Alam mo: you know

Annatto seeds: also known as achuete, red seeds used for coloring dyes or food

Arroz caldo: rice porridge with chicken

Aswang: a spirit that takes different forms to do harm to humans

Atis: soursop

Babae, babayi: female

Baby boomers: children born between 1946 and 1964

Bagoong: condiment of fermented fish, shrimp, or other seafood

Balikbayan: an expatriate visiting the Philippines

Baklava: a Middle Eastern cake

Barkada: close group of friends, a gang

Bastos: rude, impertinent

Belo: veil

Bibingka: Filipino cake made of ground rice flour or grated cassava

Bigas: husked rice

Biko: cake made of whole sweet rice

Blood meat: pork or beef stewed in its own blood

Bridge generation: American born children of pre-1965 Filipino immigrants

Chicken fight: cockfight

Compadre: godfather

Dalaga: young woman, unmarried woman

Dulce: sweets, candy

Enapoy: make fire

Flips: understood either as perjorative or colloquial for Filipino

Gabriela Silang: heroine of the Philippine Revolution against Spain

Hesusmariosep, 'susmariosep: Jesus-Mary-Joseph rapidly stated in moments of vain

Hayop: animal

Jose Rizal: Philippine national hero

Kamaganak: blood relative

Kanan: right

Kanin: cooked rice

Katipunan ng mga Demokratikong Pilipino (KDP): Union of Democratic Filipinos, a left-wing organization during the 1970's and '80's.

Kulit: repetitive, nagging

Kuya: elder brother

Lechon: roasted meat, usually a pig

Lumpia: eggroll

Mamang: mother, grandmother

Manang: elder sister

Manok: chicken, rooster

Maputla: unripe fruit, or anemic person

Maraming bata: many children

Merienda: afternoon snack

Muta: eye secretion

Nanay: mother

Nilaga: soup dish of meat and vegetables

Pai gow: Chinese card game

Pancit: noodle dish

Pangingge: old card game

Papang: father, grandfather

Pasalubong: gift

Pensionado: government sponsored college student studying in U.S.

Pinay: Filipina

Pinoy: Filipino

Pullman Porter: Stewards on passenger trains operated by the Pullman company.

Punyeta: Tagalog swear word for SOB

Puti: white

Sala: living room, family room

Sando: undershirt

Sinigang: sour soup

Sotanghon: type of noodle

Suga: tether

Tatay: father

Tiyang: aunt

Viyuda: widow

Walang kwenta: not good

Yawa: Bisayan swear word

Yuppies: young professionals

Zoot suit: fashionable suit of the 1930's

"I could almost taste the sticky rice cakes and hear the clinking of coins in 'Seven Card Stud with Seven Manangs Wild.'"

Annie Nakao, San Francisco Chronicle

"This sense that the history of Filipino Americans hasn't been fully told or recorded - leaving a growing segment of the population with only ghost images - spurred the East Bay FANHS....to tell stories about their families....(T)he past led to an anthology, a painstakingly, lovingly crafted book."

Rona Marech, San Francisco Chronicle

".....(P)romises....another cornucopia of literary delights from a sector of Philippine writing in English that continues to show the way to a new global order.....(W)hat's commendably preserved in this book is....the collective memoirs of Filipino immigrants' experience in the West Coast....(I)magine how rich a virtual cyclopedia of Fil-Am memory can help all of us....arrive at our destiny with full appreciation of all the bittersweet steps taken to get there."

Alfred A. Yuson, Philippine Daily Inquirer.